Other Kaplan Books for College Bound Students

College Admissions and Financial Aid

Access America's Guide to Studying in the USA

Guide to College Selection

High School Handbook

Kaplan/Newsweek College Catalog

Parent's Guide to College Admissions

Scholarships

What to Study: 101 Fields in a Flash

You Can Afford College

The Yale Daily News Guide to Succeeding in College

Test Preparation

ACT

ACT Essential Review

SAT & PSAT

SAT II: Biology

SAT II: Chemistry

SAT II: Mathematics

SAT II: Writing

SAT Math Workbook

SAT or ACT? Test Your Best

SAT Verbal Workbook

SAT & PSAT*

E S S E N T I A L
R E V I E W

By the Staff of
Kaplan Educational Centers

Simon & Schuster

Kaplan Books
Published by Kaplan Educational Centers and Simon & Schuster
1230 Avenue of the Americas
New York, NY 10020

Project Editor: Richard Christiano
Cover Design: Cheung Tai
Interior Page Design: gumption design
Production Editor: Maude Spekes
Desktop Publishing Manager: Michael Shevlin
Managing Editor: Brent Gallenberger
Executive Editor: Del Franz
Executive Director, Pre-College Programs: Seppy Basili

Special thanks to Maureen Blair, Marie Mockett, Kiernan McGuire, David Solomon,
and Linda Volpano.

Manufactured in the United States of America
Published Simultaneously in Canada

July 1998

10 9 8 7 6 5 4 3

ISBN: 0-684-84982-8

ISSN: 1097-5373

CONTENTS

PART FIVE: TAKING THE PSAT

APPENDIX

PREFACE

Let's face it, high school is no picnic in the park.

Chances are, you've got a lot to do between now and the day you're planning to take the SAT or PSAT. There's that killer physics exam on Friday, for example, in which you have to explain time travel. You can hardly study for that because you're the secretary of the student body and everyone's complaining about the cafeteria lunches. Your English teacher's on your case about your definition of *irony*, you're flipping burgers part-time after school, and your varsity basketball coach keeps calling to ask how the sore ankle is healing. You're rushing to classrooms, pep rallies, college admissions interviews. Wouldn't it be nice if you could use the little bits of free time you have—the odd hour here, half-hour there—to prepare for that ominous shadow looming on the horizon, the SAT or PSAT?

Well, now you can. The book you're holding in your hand right now is designed for the student who wants to prepare on the run. Here, in this convenient little volume, are gathered just about all of the most important things you need to know before walking in to these two tests. And all this information is laid out for you in 13 easy steps, so that you can learn each step fast, move on to the next activity, and get a great score when you actually take the test.

Now, don't get the wrong idea: This book won't give you comprehensive test preparation. To reach your maximum score on the SAT or PSAT will take a thorough, considered effort, and Kaplan's other books on these exams provide a more in-depth approach to taking these exams. But if you're like most busy high school students, you'll also benefit from having a portable companion to carry around—a pocket guide to basic skills, techniques, and strategies that will make you a better SAT taker. In the time it takes you to ride the bus to school every morning, you can learn the basic skills, techniques, and strategies that will make you a better SAT taker.

How much of a difference can this extra, on-the-run help make? Consider this: You can boost your score by 100 points just by getting two extra questions correct on each section! But you won't accomplish this by getting bogged down with long vocabulary lists and endless catalogues of math principles. You *can* do it by absorbing the concisely-written facts in the following pages. Through this quick, step-by-step approach, your energies will be focused on the essential elements of the exam—places where you can really boost your score easily, and fast.

For instance, you'll see the top eight math traps that appear again and again on the SAT. In a couple of hours, you can learn how to avoid these traps and improve your math score significantly. Similarly, Kaplan has developed some easy methods for figuring out the meanings of unfamiliar vocabulary words, so that you can pile up verbal points even if you've never heard of the words in the question.

So don't panic. Maybe you do need 25 hours in a day to get everything done. But with *SAT & PSAT Essential Review* in hand, it's not too late to get in some solid preparation for these tests. If you've got a few spare hours a week, you still have a chance to boost your score.

HOW TO USE THIS BOOK

The study program for this book is divided into 13 distinct "steps." Each step is centered around a vital area of SAT techniques, with the introductory step in Part One, Verbal steps grouped together in Part Two, Math steps in Part Three, and the steps for putting it all together in Part Four. The special skills you'll need for the PSAT are covered in Part Five. Each step should take you an hour or two to review, but feel free to skim the steps you feel confident of so that you can spend more time on the ones you feel shaky on. The 13 steps vary in length, but they're all important to your score, so make sure you at least have a look at each one.

QUICK POINTS

Scattered throughout each step are various "Quick Points"—one-sentence summaries of the major tips and strategies covered in the step. It's extremely important that you learn these points, which is why we've set them off in the text with the following icon.

 DRESS IN LAYERS ON TEST DAY. YOU CAN'T PREDICT HOW COMFORTABLE THE EXAM ROOM WILL BE, AND ANY DISTRACTION—NO MATTER HOW TRIVIAL—CAN COST YOU POINTS.

Also set off from the body of the text are various other hints, pointers, and warnings that you should pay close attention to.

STEP RECAPS

At the end of each step, you'll find a section called "Step Recap." Here, to save you time, we've gathered together all of that step's Quick Points in a single place. Review these recap sections frequently to imprint these important points on your brain. You should also review these recaps at the end of your study program, a day or so before the test. If you remember nothing else on Test Day, remember these points.

POP QUIZZES

At the end of many steps there will also be a "Pop Quiz" testing you on the material covered in that step. Try to complete these quizzes within the time limits shown, which reflect the timings for these questions on the actual SAT and PSAT. Part of the trick of doing well on these tests is performing well under time pressure, so be strict with your stopwatch!

Using these study aids will help you focus your time and energies so that you can get the best possible score improvement in the time left to you.

KAPLAN

PART ONE

AN INTRODUCTION TO THE SAT

STEP 1:
A CRASH COURSE IN
SAT KNOW-HOW

KNOWING THY ENEMY

To perform well on the SAT, you need to draw on a skill that isn't mentioned in any of the College Board's materials: You need to be a good test taker.

How do you acquire this skill? Quite simply, you must learn to think like the test maker.

Every time you meet someone new, it takes you a little while to adjust to and understand that person's behavior. Similarly, you need to understand the SAT's personality. You need to know what forms of communication the SAT understands—mathematics and the English language. You need to know how to think when dealing with the SAT, and which strategies work best. Finally, you need to become familiar with the test's method of operation . . . in essence, how it thinks.

Kaplan has devoted many hours and resources to understanding the SAT and to figuring out what you need to perform well on it. The knowledge gained through that effort is reflected in the books Kaplan publishes about the exam, and this book presents the most important facts you need to know in a concise, distilled form.

 3

WHAT IS THE SAT?

The SAT is a three-hour, mostly multiple-choice exam that is divided into seven sections. These sections can appear in any order:

- Two 30-minute Verbal sections with Analogies, Sentence Completions, and Critical Reading
- One 15-minute Verbal section with Critical Reading
- One 30-minute Math section with Quantitative Comparisons and Grid-ins
- One 30-minute Math section with regular Math
- One 15-minute Math section with regular Math
- One 30-minute experimental section (Math or Verbal)

The experimental section is used by the test makers to try out new questions and does not affect your score. It can show up anywhere on the exam and will look like any Verbal or Math section. Don't try to figure out which section is experimental and then skip it—the odds are against your guessing correctly, and even if you do figure it out, the effort will make you lose your momentum.

There are six types of questions on the SAT: three Verbal types and three Math types. The likely number of questions you'll see of each type is listed in the following pie charts:

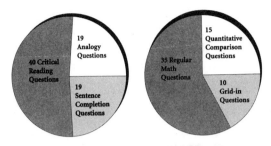

Don't worry about the specifics of these question types just yet; they'll be explained in more detail later in upcoming chapters.

WHAT ABOUT THE PSAT?

The PSAT, or Preliminary SAT, is similar to the SAT in content and structure. Consequently, all of the strategies discussed in this book also apply to the PSAT. However, the PSAT is different from the SAT in one respect: It includes a Writing Skills section. To help you score higher on this section, we've developed a chapter that provides the content review, skills, and strategies you'll need. Also covered is important information on test format, scoring, and National Merit scholarships.

HOW IS THE SAT SCORED?

You get one point for each correct answer on the SAT and lose a fraction of a point for each wrong answer (except in Grid-ins, where you lose nothing for a wrong answer). Questions left blank do not affect your score one way or the other. The totals for the 78 Verbal and 60 Math questions are added up to produce two raw scores. These, however, are not your final SAT scores.

After the raw scores are calculated, they are converted into scaled scores with 200 as the lowest score, and 800 the highest. These scaled scores are the numbers reported to you and to the colleges you choose.

The final digit of your scaled score will always be a 0. This means that your score is measured in increments of 10; making it impossible to get scores like 492 or 376. How does ETS convert your raw score to a scaled score? The method varies from test to test, but each raw point is worth approximately 10 scaled points.

THE SAT IS PREDICTABLE

Put yourself in the test maker's shoes for a moment. You must make certain that the students tested in June have a similar experience to the students tested in November. How do you accomplish this? First, you must make sure that the test is as standardized and predictable as possible—there can't be any surprises.

Of course, you can't use the same questions over and over. But you can use the same question types to create new questions according to specific guidelines.

Now put your student shoes back on and think about this for a moment: The test maker's predictability works to your advantage, and for several reasons. The first thing working in your favor is that the directions to the questions will always be the same.

KNOW THE DIRECTIONS

One of the easiest things you can do to help your performance on the SAT is to understand the directions before taking the test. Since the instructions are always exactly the same, there's no reason to waste your time reading them on the day of the test. Learn them beforehand, as you go through this book, so you can skip them Test Day.

DIFFICULTY FOLLOWS A STANDARD

What else is predictable on the SAT? You've probably noticed that some SAT questions are more difficult than others. Except for the Critical Reading problems, the questions are generally designed to get tougher as you work through a set.

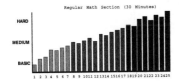

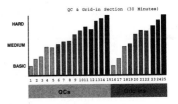

Notice that in the graph on the right, the difficulty level builds to a peak, then falls drastically to the "basic" level, and then starts building again. This is because the difficulty pattern starts over again each time a new question type begins (except for Critical Reading). In other words, if a section begins with a set of Analogy questions, those questions will begin with an easy one and then gradually become more difficult. Then, if the section proceeds to a set of Sentence Completion questions, this set will also progress from easy to difficult.

WHY DOES DIFFICULTY MATTER?

How can you use the difficulty pattern to your advantage? As you work, you should always be aware of where you are in a set. When working on the easy problems, you can generally trust your first impulse—the obvious answer is likely to be right.

As you get to the end of the set, you need to become more suspicious because the answers probably won't come easy. If they do, look at the problem again because the obvious answer is likely to be wrong. Watch out for the answer that "just looks right." It may be a distractor—a wrong answer choice meant to entice you.

WHAT MAKES A HARD QUESTION HARD?

A hard question is hard not because it deals with difficult material—you won't be asked about Einstein's theory of relativity. Hard questions are tough for two reasons: (1) Their answers are not immediately obvious, and (2) the questions do not ask for information in a straightforward manner.

Here is an easy question.

> Known for their devotion, dogs were often used as symbols of _____ in Medieval and Renaissance painting.
>
> (A) breakfast
>
> (B) tidal waves
>
> (C) fidelity
>
> (D) campfires
>
> (E) toothpaste

KAPLAN

The correct answer, fidelity (C), probably leapt right out at you. This question was a little too easy and would never appear on the actual SAT. But we exaggerated the question a bit to make a point. Easy questions are purposely designed to be easy and their answer choices are purposely made obvious.

Now here is virtually the same question, made difficult.

> Known for their _____, dogs were often used as symbols of _____ in Medieval and Renaissance painting.
>
> (A) dispassion . . bawdiness
>
> (B) fidelity . . aloofness
>
> (C) monogamy . . parsimony
>
> (D) parity . . diplomacy
>
> (E) loyalty . . faithfulness

See the difference? This time the answer was harder to find. For one thing, the answer choices were far more difficult. In addition, the sentence contained two blanks.

The correct answer is (E). Did you fall for (B) because the first word is *fidelity*? (B) is a good example of a distractor. But don't sweat it. By the time you are done with this book, a question like this will be a piece of cake because you will know how to attack it.

MOVE AROUND

So what have you learned now that you can identify the difference between a hard and easy problem? Simple: Easy problems are worth as many points as tough problems, so do the easy problems first. Don't rush through the easy problems just to get to the hard ones, however; you don't want to make any careless errors. When you run into questions that look tough, circle them in your test booklet and skip them for the time being. (Make sure you skip them on your answer grid too.)

Remember, the name of the game is to get as many points as possible. To that end, you need to score points as quickly as possible. Feel free to move around within a section to rack up those points, but remember that you can't skip from section to section. And always be careful to fill in ovals that correspond to the question you're answering. It may sound obvious, but if you skip around within a section you're more likely to *misgrid,* or fill in an oval whose answer corresponds to a different question than the one you intended to answer.

THE PROCESS OF ELIMINATION

Okay, so now you know a little bit about how the test is structured. Here's a tip about how you should approach each question. Sometimes it is not immediately obvious which answer is the correct one. In that case, you should eliminate unreasonable answer choices. Take a look at this question again.

> Known for their devotion, dogs were often used as symbols of _____ in Medieval and Renaissance painting.
>
> (A) breakfast
>
> (B) tidal waves
>
> (C) fidelity
>
> (D) campfires
>
> (E) toothpaste

Chances are, you recognized that choice (A), *breakfast*, was wrong. You then looked at the next answer choice, and then the next one, and so on. In other words, you eliminated wrong answers to find the correct answer. Often, this process is the best way to work through the SAT. This book will show you ways to immediately identify answer choices that you can eliminate.

GUESSING IS GOOD

What happens if you can't eliminate four out of five answer choices? Should you guess? Should you skip the question? What about the penalty for guessing?

The test makers like to talk about the guessing penalty on the SAT. This is a misnomer because it's really a wrong-answer penalty. If you guess wrong, you get penalized. But if you guess right, you score points.

The fact is, if you can eliminate one or more answers as definitely wrong, you'll turn the odds in your favor and actually come out ahead by guessing.

Here's how the penalty works:

- If you get an answer wrong on a Quantitative Comparison question, which has four answer choices, you lose one third of a point.
- If you get an answer wrong on the other multiple-choice questions, which have five answer choices, you lose one-fourth of a point.
- If you get an answer wrong on a Math Grid-in question, for which you write in your own answers, you lose nothing.

The fractional points you lose are meant to offset the points you might score "accidentally" by guessing the correct answer. But here's a better way to think about it.

Let's say that for every question you answer correctly, you receive one dollar. If you miss the question, you lose 25 cents.

Now, out of five questions with five answer choices each, the odds are that you will answer one question correctly and get the other four wrong. This means that you will receive one dollar, but since you have to pay out a dollar for the wrong answers; you have a net gain of zero.

But what happens when you eliminate one of the answer choices for each question? Now you have a one-in-four chance of answering each question correctly. That means out of four questions, you will receive one dollar and pay out 75 cents. That's a net gain of 25 cents. Imagine the profit you'll make over the course of an entire exam.

The bottom line is, if you can eliminate one or more answers as definitely incorrect, you must guess.

PACING

The SAT gives you a lot of questions in a short period of time. To get through a whole section, you can't spend too much time on any one question. Keep moving through the test at a good speed; if you run into a hard question, circle it in your test booklet, skip it, and come back to it later if you have time.

The recommended average times per question follow:

Recommended Timing

Question Type	On Average
Analogies	30 Seconds
Sentence Completions	30 Seconds
Critical Reading*	75 Seconds
Regular Math	70 Seconds
QCs	40 Seconds
Grid-ins	120 Seconds

*Average time for Critical Reading includes time to read the passage. Spend about 40 seconds per question.

This doesn't mean that you should spend exactly 30 seconds on every Analogy. The chart is just a guide. Remember, the questions get harder as you move through a problem set. Ideally, you can work through the easy problems at a brisk, steady clip and use a little more of your time for the harder ones that come at the end of the set.

The Answer Grid Has No Heart

Once again, it sounds simple but it's extremely important: Don't make mistakes filling out your answer grid! When time is short it's easy to get confused, going back and forth between your test book and your grid. If you misgrid one question, you can misgrid several others before realizing your error—if you realize it at all. You can lose a lot of points this way.

To avoid mistakes on the answer grid:

Always Circle the Questions You Skip

Put a big circle in your test book around the number of any question you skip, so they'll be easy to locate when you return to them. Also, if you realize later that you accidentally skipped a box on the grid, you can more easily check your grid against your book to see where you went wrong.

Always Circle the Answers You Choose

Circling your answers in the test book also makes it easier to check your grid against your book.

Grid Five or More Answers at Once

Don't transfer your answers to the grid after every question. Transfer your answers after every five questions, or at the end of each reading passage. (*Exception:* When time is running out at the end of a section, start gridding one by one so you don't get caught at the end with ungridded answers!) That way, you won't keep breaking your concentration to mark the grid. You'll save time and improve accuracy.

Write in Your Booklet

Finally, remember that the SAT is something you have paid to take; don't be afraid to mark up your test booklet. Even though proctors collect booklets at the end of each testing session, the booklets are not examined or re-used. So use the space the test makers give you to find those correct answers and gain points.

STEP ONE RECAP

- Don't try to guess which section is experimental.
- Learn the directions before Test Day.
- You are allowed to move around within a section, but don't misgrid.
- Skip questions that look difficult or time consuming. Return to them later if you have time.
- On easy questions, the correct answer is obvious.
- On hard questions, the obvious answer is probably wrong.
- Don't let distractor answer choices lead you astray.
- Use the process of elimination to isolate the correct answer.
- When you can eliminate more than one answer as definitely incorrect, go ahead and guess.
- Be aware of where you are in each section and pace yourself accordingly.
- Circle the questions you skip.
- Circle the answers you choose.
- Grid five or more answers at once.
- Don't be afraid to mark up your test booklet.

PART TWO

VERBAL

STEP 2:
BASIC VERBAL STRATEGIES

SAT VERBAL ISN'T THE SUM OF ALL KNOWLEDGE ABOUT LANGUAGE

Linguists spend their entire lives studying the intricacies of language. But you don't have a lifetime to prepare for SAT Verbal: You have a week. Well, don't sweat it. There's a world of things about language that the test makers do not care about. The SAT, for instance, doesn't test spelling or grammar. It doesn't test your knowledge of English literature or literary terms. It will never ask you to interpret a poem. No, SAT Verbal covers a fairly predictable, fairly limited body of skills and knowledge: vocabulary, verbal reasoning, and reading skills. You can boost your score with just the material presented here.

HOW SAT VERBAL IS SET UP

There are three scored Verbal sections on the SAT. The breakdown of the questions goes like this:

PART TWO: Verbal

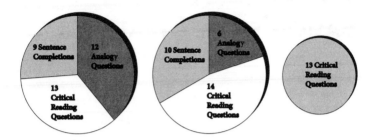

- One 30-minute section with 9 Sentence Completions, 13 Analogies, and 13 Critical Reading questions.
- One 30-minute section with 10 Sentence Completions, 6 Analogies, and 14 Critical Reading questions.
- One 15-minute section with 13 Critical Reading questions.

The Sentence Completions and Analogies are arranged in order of difficulty. The first few questions in a set are meant to be fairly straightforward and manageable. The middle few questions will be a little harder, and the last few are the most difficult. Keep this in mind as you work.

Critical Reading is not arranged by difficulty. Whenever you find yourself beginning to spend too much time on a question, you should skip it and return to it later.

> ☞ LEARN THE VERBAL QUESTION TYPES NOW SO YOU DON'T HAVE TO FIGURE THEM OUT ON TEST DAY.

HOW TO APPROACH SAT VERBAL

To do well on SAT Verbal, you need to be systematic in your approach to each question type and each of the three Verbal sections. Sentence Completions and Analogies are designed to be done relatively quickly. That means you can earn points fast, so you should do these first. Critical Reading takes a lot longer, so you can't just leave yourself five minutes to do a passage. *Remember, you earn just as many points for an easy question as you do for a hard one.*

TAPPING YOUR SAT VERBAL SKILLS

Doing your best on SAT Verbal comes from knowing what to expect and knowing that you have the skills to handle it. You use words every day. You make your own ideas clear, and you understand and respond to those of others. In all of these cases—talking with friends or talking with teachers, reading a textbook or reading a billboard, listening to lyrics or listening to your SAT proctor's instructions—you take in limited information, process it through your own intellect and experience, and make sense of it. If you can learn to make the most of these skills, you can improve your Verbal score.

Here's how to apply those general points to the specifics of the SAT Verbal sections.

VOCABULARY

You know how to read. You can explain the relationship between *kitten* and *cat* to a three-year-old. So what makes the Verbal section such a challenge? Vocabulary. You may have a solid understanding of a Critical Reading passage but then get thrown by one tough vocabulary word. You may know the relationship between the original pair of words in an Analogy, but have a tough time finding the answer because all the choices have words you've never seen before. You may know precisely what kind of word to fill in on a Sentence Completion, and then find that all the answer choices look like they're in a foreign language.

All three Verbal question types—Analogies, Sentence Completions, and Critical Reading—depend on your ability to work with unfamiliar words. You won't be asked to define words on the SAT. But you'll need to have a sense of their meaning in order to answer the questions.

There are two types of hard SAT words:

- Unfamiliar words
- Familiar words with unfamiliar meanings

Some words are hard because you haven't seen them before. The words *scintilla* or *circumlocution*, for instance, are probably not part of your everyday vocabulary. But they just might pop up on your SAT.

Easy words, like *recognize* or *appreciation*, may also trip you up on Test Day because they have secondary meanings that you aren't used to. Analogies and Critical Reading in particular will throw you familiar words with unfamiliar meanings.

Those who prepare for the SAT months ahead of time study word roots and word lists to sharpen their vocabularies. But you can take a shortcut and get similar results. Here's how.

DECODING STRANGE WORDS ON TEST DAY

Trying to learn every word that could possibly appear on the SAT is like trying to memorize the license-plate number of every car on the freeway. It's not much fun, it'll give you a headache, and you probably won't pull it off.

Even if you were to spend hours with flash cards, vocabulary tapes, and word lists, you'd be bound to face some mystery words on your SAT. No big deal. Just as you can use your basic multiplication skills to find the product of even the largest numbers, you can use what you know about words to focus on likely meanings of tough vocabulary words.

GO WITH YOUR HUNCHES

When you look at an unfamiliar word, your first reaction may be to say, "Don't know it. Gotta skip it." *Not so fast.* Vocabulary knowledge on the SAT is not an all-or-nothing proposition.

- Some words you know so well you can rattle off a dictionary definition of them.
- Some words you sort of know. You understand them when you see them in context, but don't feel confident using them yourself.
- Some words are vaguely familiar. You know you've heard them somewhere before.

1. Try to Recall Where You've Heard the Word Before

If you can recall a phrase in which the word appears, that may be enough to eliminate some answer choices, or even to zero in on the right answer. Let's try a sample question.

> Between the two villages was a deep - - - - through which passage was difficult and hazardous.
>
> (A) precipice
>
> (B) beachhead
>
> (C) quagmire
>
> (D) market
>
> (E) prairie

To answer this question, it helps to know the word *quagmire*. You may remember *quagmire* from news reports referring to "a foreign policy quagmire" or "a quagmire of financial indebtedness." If you can remember how "quagmire" was used, you'll have a rough idea of what it means, and you'll see it fits.

 IF YOU THINK YOU RECOGNIZE A WORD, GO WITH YOUR HUNCH.

You may also be reminded of the word *mire*, as in "We got mired in the small details and never got to the larger issue." Sounds something like "stuck," right? You don't need an exact definition. A quagmire is a situation that's difficult to get out of, so (C) is correct. (Literally, a quagmire is a soft, spongy, easy-to-get-stuck-in piece of land.)

USE COMMON WORD ASSOCIATIONS AND PHRASES TO UNLOCK DIFFICULT WORDS.

2. Decide if the Word Has a Positive or Negative "Charge"

Simply knowing that you're dealing with a positive or negative word can earn you points on the SAT.

Look at the word *cantankerous*. Say it to yourself. Can you guess whether it's positive or negative? Often words that sound harsh have a negative meaning while smooth-sounding words tend to have positive meanings. If *cantankerous* sounded negative to you, you were right. It means "disagreeable" or "difficult to deal with."

You can also use prefixes and roots to help determine a word's charge. *Mal-, de-, dis-, un-, in-, im-, a-,* and *mis-* often indicate a negative, while *pro-, ben-,* and *magn-* are often positives—so work these into the context of a question.

Not all SAT words sound positive or negative; some sound neutral. But if you can define the charge, you can probably eliminate some answer choices on that basis alone.

 TRUST YOUR SENSE OF AN UNFAMILIAR WORD'S "CHARGE."

He seemed at first to be honest and loyal, but before long it was necessary to - - - - him for his - - - - behavior.

(A)   admonish . . steadfast

(B)   extol . . conniving

(C)   reprimand . . scrupulous

(D)   exalt . . insidious

(E)   castigate . . perfidious

You don't need an exact definition of the words that go in the blanks. The word *but* tells you all you need to know—that the words for both blanks have to be negative (to contrast with the positive words *honest* and *loyal*). So you scan the answer choices for a choice that contains two clearly negative words. (E) is right. *Castigate* means "punish or scold harshly," and *perfidious* means "disloyal" or "treacherous."

3. Use Your Foreign-Language Skills

Many of the roots you'll encounter in SAT words come from Latin. Spanish, French, and Italian also come from Latin, and have retained much of it in their modern forms. English is also a cousin to German and Greek. So if you don't recognize a word, you should try to remember if you know a similar word in another language.

Look at the word *carnal*. Unfamiliar? What about *carne*, as in *chili con carne*? *Carn* means "meat" or "flesh," which leads you straight to the meaning of *carnal*: "pertaining to the flesh." You could decode *carnivorous*, or meat eating, in the same way.

 LOOK FOR WORD ELEMENTS YOU KNOW FROM FOREIGN LANGUAGES.

4. When All Else Fails . . .

Eliminate choices that are clearly wrong and make an educated guess from the remaining choices.

- A wrong answer won't hurt you much.
- A right answer will help you a lot.

SOME CHOICES ON VERBAL QUESTIONS WILL JUST SOUND WRONG. IF YOU CAN ELIMINATE AT LEAST ONE WRONG-SOUNDING CHOICE, YOU IMPROVE YOUR CHANCES OF A CORRECT GUESS.

STEP TWO RECAP

- Learn the verbal question types now so you don't have to figure them out on Test Day.
- If you think you recognize a word, go with your hunch.
- Use common word associations and phrases to unlock difficult words.
- Trust your sense of an unfamiliar word's "charge."
- Look for word elements you know from foreign languages.
- Some choices on verbal questions will just sound wrong. If you can eliminate at least one wrong-sounding choice, you improve your chances of guessing correctly.

STEP 3:
ANALOGY TECHNIQUES

ANALOGIES ARE NOT A DISEASE

Analogies may seem frightening at first because they don't look like anything you've ever done before. But once you get familiar with the format, you'll find there's a simple method for mastering this question type. In fact, short-term prepping often gains you more points on Analogies than on any other Verbal question type. You can even learn to get an Analogy right when you don't know the meaning of all the words.

> *STATISTIC: The 19 Analogies count for about one-fourth of your Verbal score.*

THE FORMAT

There are 19 Analogies on the SAT, and they are among the quickest questions on the test. You'll probably see one set of thirteen and one set of six. Each 30-minute Verbal section contains a set of Analogies. The directions will read something like the following.

> Choose the lettered pair of words that is related in the same way as the pair in capital letters.
>
> FLAKE : SNOW ::
>
> (A)   storm : hail
>
> (B)   drop : rain
>
> (C)   field : wheat
>
> (D)   stack : hay
>
> (E)   cloud : fog
>
> (A) (B) (C) (D) (E)

The key to the instructions is the word *related*. Your job is to figure out which pair of words among your choices has the same relationship as the pair of stem words (the words in capital letters). In this example, the answer is (B). A FLAKE is a small unit of SNOW, just as a drop is a small unit of rain.

BUILD BRIDGES

In every Analogy question, there is a strong, definite connection between the two stem words. Your task is to identify this relationship and then look for a similar relationship among the answer pairs.

What makes a strong, definite relationship?

- The words *library* and *book* have a strong, definite connection. A library is defined as a place where books are kept. LIBRARY : BOOK could be a question stem.
- The words *library* and *child*, on the other hand, do not have a strong, definite connection. A child may or may not have anything to do with a library. LIBRARY : CHILD would probably not be a question stem.

The best way to pinpoint the relationship between the stem words is to "build a bridge." A bridge is a short sentence that relates the two words. Often, a bridge reads like a definition of one of the two words. For instance: "A LIBRARY is a place where BOOKS are kept."

The ability to make up such sentences—to build bridges—is fundamental to Analogy success. Your bridge needs to capture the strong, definite connection between the words.

 ALWAYS BUILD A BRIDGE BETWEEN ANALOGY STEM WORDS.

KAPLAN'S THREE-STEP METHOD FOR ANALOGIES

1. Build a bridge between the stem words.
2. Plug in the answer choices.
3. Adjust your bridge, if necessary.

PART TWO: Verbal

Here's an Analogy stem. We've left out the answer choices because you need to focus first on the stem.

LILY : FLOWER ::

1. Build a Bridge

The best bridge here is "A LILY is a type of FLOWER."

2. Plug in the Answer Choices

Here is the complete question:

LILY : FLOWER ::

- (A) rose : thorn
- (B) cocoon : butterfly
- (C) brick : building
- (D) maple : tree
- (E) sky : airplane

Take your bridge and plug in answer choices (A) through (E). If only one pair fits, it's the answer.

> *HINT: Be sure to try all five choices. And don't be distracted by choices whose subject resembles that of the stem words. Unless the pair in the choice has the same relationship as the stem pair, it's wrong.*

Here's how plugging in the answer choices works:

(A) A rose is a type of thorn? No.

(B) A cocoon is a type of butterfly? No.

(C) A brick is a type of building? No.

(D) A maple is a type of tree? Yes.

(E) A sky is a type of airplane? No.

Since only one choice fits our bridge, the answer is clearly (D).

3. Adjust Your Bridge, If Necessary

If no answer choice seems to fit, your bridge is too specific, and you should go back and adjust it. If more than one answer choice fits, your bridge is not specific enough. Look at this example:

SNAKE : SLITHER ::

   (A)   egg : hatch

   (B)   wolf : howl

   (C)   rabbit : hop

   (D)   turtle : snap

   (E)   tarantula : bite

With a simple bridge, such as "A SNAKE SLITHERs," you'd be hard pressed to find the answer. All the answer choices make sense: An egg hatches; a wolf howls; a rabbit hops; a turtle snaps; a tarantula bites. Go back to step one and build another bridge, this time making it more specific. Think about what SLITHER means.

New bridge: A SNAKE SLITHERs to get around.

(A) An egg hatches to get around? No.

(B) A wolf howls to get around? No.

(C) A rabbit hops to get around? Yes.

(D) A turtle snaps to get around? No.

(E) A tarantula bites to get around? No.

Four *no* answers and one *yes:* The answer is (C).

> HINT: *If no answer fits, build a broader bridge; if too many fit, build a narrower bridge. Remember, only one answer choice should be able to "go across" the bridge.*

WHAT PART OF SPEECH IS A STEM WORD?

Occasionally, you might have to take a quick peek at the answer choices before you can build a bridge for the stem. The part of speech of a stem word may be ambiguous. When you're not sure whether a stem word is a noun, a verb, an adjective, or an adverb, look at the words directly beneath that stem word.

> HINT: *The words in a vertical row are all the same part of speech.*

For example, you might see this:

VERB: NOUN ::

    (A) verb : noun

    (B) verb :noun

    (C) verb : noun

    (D) verb : noun

    (E) verb : noun

But on an SAT Analogy, you'll never see this:

NOUN : NOUN ::

(A) verb : noun

(B) noun : noun

(C) verb : verb

(D) verb : noun

(E) verb : noun

To establish a stem word's part of speech, you don't usually have to look at more than one or two choices.

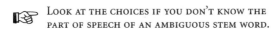 LOOK AT THE CHOICES IF YOU DON'T KNOW THE PART OF SPEECH OF AN AMBIGUOUS STEM WORD.

How would you think through the following example?

PINE : DESIRE ::

(A) laugh : sorrow

(B) drink : thirst

(C) watch : interest

(D) listen : awe

(E) starve : hunger

The first thing you think of when you read PINE is the tree. But you can't build a bridge between a tree with needlelike leaves and DESIRE. So PINE has to be another part of speech. A glance at the answer choices below PINE (*laugh, drink, watch, listen,* and *starve*) tells you that PINE is being used as a verb (since *listen* and *starve* can only be verbs).

What about DESIRE? It could be a noun or a verb, but the answer choices beneath it (*sorrow, thirst, interest, awe,* and *hunger*) tell you it's used as a noun.

You've probably heard of someone pining away from unrequited love. As a verb, PINE means "to yearn or suffer from longing." A good bridge would be "to PINE is to suffer from extreme DESIRE." Plugging in the answer choices, you get:

(A) To laugh is to suffer from extreme sorrow? No.

(B) To drink is to suffer from extreme thirst? No.

(C) To watch is to suffer from extreme interest? No.

(D) To listen is to suffer from extreme awe? No.

(E) To starve is to suffer from extreme hunger? Yes.

Once again, four *no*s and one *yes*; the answer is (E).

 USE KAPLAN'S THREE-STEP METHOD FOR ANALOGIES:
1. BUILD A BRIDGE.
2. PLUG IN THE ANSWER CHOICES.
3. ADJUST YOUR BRIDGE, IF NECESSARY.

NINE CLASSIC BRIDGES

It's easier to build bridges when you know the types of bridges that have appeared on the SAT in the past. While no one can give you a list of the words that will appear on SAT Analogies, you can learn what types of relationships to expect. The classic bridges below appear repeatedly on the SAT.

> *HINT: Learn to recognize common types of bridges that connect stem words on the SAT. They can speed you to the right answer.*

Classic bridges may take different forms, depending on what parts of speech are used. But the underlying concepts are what matter. Here are examples of nine classic types. Try to know these, or at least learn to recognize them, by Test Day.

Bridge Type #1: DESCRIPTION

In many Analogies, one stem word is a person, place, or thing, and the other word is a characteristic of that person, place, or thing. Look at these examples:

> PAUPER : POOR—A PAUPER is always POOR.

> GENIUS : INTELLIGENT—A GENIUS is always INTELLIGENT.

This classic bridge can also describe a person, place, or thing by what it is *not*.

> PAUPER:WEALTHY—A PAUPER is never WEALTHY.

> GENIUS:STUPID—A GENIUS is never STUPID.

TRY IT YOURSELF

Here are more classic bridges. Fill in each blank with a stem word that will complete the bridge. There may be more than one way to fill in each blank. The important thing is to get the right idea.

Bridge Type #2: CHARACTERISTIC ACTIONS

An INSOMNIAC can't ———.

A GLUTTON likes to ———.

Bridge Type #3: LACK

Something MURKY lacks ———.

A PESSIMIST lacks ———.

Bridge Type #4: CATEGORIES

MEASLES is a type of ———.

A BARRACUDA is a type of ———.

Bridge Type #5: SIZE/DEGREE

To SPEAK very quietly is to ———.

To LIKE strongly is to ———.

Bridge Type #6: CAUSING/STOPPING

A REMEDY stops or cures an ———.

An OBSTACLE prevents ———.

Bridge Type #7: PLACES

A JUDGE works in a ———.

A PLAY is performed on a ———.

Bridge Type #8: FUNCTION

GILLS are used for ———.

A PAINTBRUSH is used to ———.

Bridge Type #9: PART/WHOLE

An ARMY is made up of ————.

A CROWD is made up of many ————.

SUGGESTED ANSWERS TO BRIDGE TYPES

Your answers may vary from our suggested answers. As long as you recognized the relationship, that's okay.

Characteristic Actions

An INSOMNIAC can't SLEEP.

A GLUTTON likes to EAT.

Lack

Something MURKY lacks CLARITY.

A PESSIMIST lacks HOPE.

Categories

MEASLES is a type of ILLNESS.

A BARRACUDA is a type of FISH.

Size/Degree

To SPEAK very quietly is to WHISPER.

To LIKE strongly is to LOVE (or ADORE).

Causing/Stopping

A REMEDY stops or cures an ILLNESS.

An OBSTACLE prevents PROGRESS (or PASSAGE).

Places

A JUDGE works in a COURTROOM.

A PLAY is performed on a STAGE (or in a THEATER).

Function

GILLS are used for BREATHING.

A PAINTBRUSH is used to PAINT.

Part/Whole

An ARMY is made up of SOLDIERS.

A CROWD is made up of many PEOPLE.

 LEARN TO RECOGNIZE THE CLASSIC TYPES OF BRIDGES USED IN ANALOGY QUESTIONS.

Now that you've got a handle on Analogies, try the following Pop Quiz.

ANALOGY POP QUIZ

Answer 10 questions (5 minutes). Choose the lettered pair of words that is related in the same way as the pair in capital letters.

1.   COPPER : METAL ::

   (A) grain : sand

   (B) helium : gas

   (C) stem : flower

   (D) tree : trunk

   (E) stone : clay

   Ⓐ Ⓑ Ⓒ Ⓓ Ⓔ

2.   BROOM : DIRT ::

   (A) brush : bristles

   (B) fork : plate

   (C) rake : leaves

   (D) mirror : face

   (E) scissors : blades

   Ⓐ Ⓑ Ⓒ Ⓓ Ⓔ

3.   COWARD : BRAVERY::

   (A) eccentric : conformity

   (B) hero : fortitude

   (C) prophet : vision

   (D) sage : wisdom

   (E) comedian : humor

   Ⓐ Ⓑ Ⓒ Ⓓ Ⓔ

PART TWO: Verbal

4. REVERE : ADMIRE ::
    (A) cherish : conceive
    (B) release : reject
    (C) guess : solve
    (D) propose : change
    (E) despise : disdain

    $\textcircled{A}$ $\textcircled{B}$ $\textcircled{C}$ $\textcircled{D}$ $\textcircled{E}$

5. PERPLEXING : CONFUSION::
    (A) appalling : dismay
    (B) static : change
    (C) unpleasant : chaos
    (D) dignified : pride
    (E) grave : regret

    $\textcircled{A}$ $\textcircled{B}$ $\textcircled{C}$ $\textcircled{D}$ $\textcircled{E}$

6. AMUSING : MIRTH ::
    (A) ailing : health
    (B) painful : sympathy
    (C) optimistic : objectivity
    (D) protective : insecurity
    (E) terrifying : fear

    $\textcircled{A}$ $\textcircled{B}$ $\textcircled{C}$ $\textcircled{D}$ $\textcircled{E}$

7. FOOD : MENU ::

    (A) accounting : inventory

    (B) index : foreword

    (C) silverware : spoon

    (D) merchandise : catalogue

    (E) films : credits

    Ⓐ Ⓑ Ⓒ Ⓓ Ⓔ

8. IMPERCEPTIBLE : DETECT ::

    (A) fundamental : begin

    (B) inconceivable : imagine

    (C) rugged : seize

    (D) costly : overcharge

    (E) immense : notice

    Ⓐ Ⓑ Ⓒ Ⓓ Ⓔ

9. PERSEVERE : DOGGED ::

    (A) comply : obedient

    (B) inspire : pompous

    (C) hesitate : reckless

    (D) speak : laconic

    (E) retard : expeditious

    Ⓐ Ⓑ Ⓒ Ⓓ Ⓔ

10. ENTHRALLING : TEDIUM ::
    (A) witty : frivolity
    (B) insipid : appetite
    (C) glaring : illumination
    (D) wearisome : redundancy
    (E) trite : originality

EXPLANATIONS

1. (B)
Copper is a kind of metal.

2. (C)
A broom is used to clear away dirt.

3. (A)
A coward does not display bravery.

4. (E)
To revere is to admire very much.

5. (A)
Something that is perplexing causes confusion.

6. (E)
Something that is amusing causes mirth.

7. (D)
A menu is a list of available food.

8. (B)
If something is imperceptible, you cannot detect it.

9. (A)
A dogged person is one who perseveres.

10. (E)
Something that is enthralling lacks tedium.

STEP THREE RECAP

- Always build a bridge between Analogy stem words.
- Look at the choices if you don't know the part of speech of an ambiguous stem word.
- Use Kaplan's Three-Step Method for Analogies:
  1. Build a bridge.
  2. Plug in the answer choices.
  3. Adjust your bridge, if necessary.
- Learn to recognize the classic types of bridges used in Analogy questions.

Step 4:
Sentence Completions
Techniques

Filling In the Blanks

Of all the Verbal question types, Sentence Completions are probably the most student-friendly. Unlike Analogies, they give you some context in which to think about vocabulary words, and unlike Critical Reading, they only require you to pay attention to a single sentence at a time.

STATISTIC: The 19 Sentence Completions count for about one-fourth of your Verbal score.

19
Sentence
Completions

THE FORMAT

There are 19 Sentence Completions in all on the SAT. You'll probably see one set of nine and one set of ten. They appear in both 30-minute Verbal sections. The instructions for Sentence Completions look something like this:

Select the lettered word or set of words that best completes the sentence.

Today's small, portable computers contrast markedly with the earliest electronic computers, which were - - - - .

    (A) effective

    (B) invented

    (C) useful

    (D) destructive

    (E) enormous

In the example, the new computers, which are small and portable, are contrasted with old computers. You can infer that the old computers must have been the opposite of small and portable, so (E), enormous, is right.

KAPLAN'S FOUR-STEP METHOD FOR SENTENCE COMPLETIONS

Here's the basic method for Sentence Completions.

1. Read the Sentence Carefully

Think about the sentence before looking at the various answer choices. Figure out what the sentence means, taking special note of the clue words. A word like *but* tells you to expect a contrast coming up; a word like "moreover" tells you that what follows is a continuation of the same idea.

 CLUE WORDS LIKE *AND, BUT, SUCH AS,* AND *ALTHOUGH* TELL YOU HOW THE PARTS OF A SENTENCE RELATE TO EACH OTHER.

2. Predict the Answer

Anticipate the words that go in the blanks. Do this before looking at the answer choices.

> *HINT: You don't have to make an exact prediction. A rough idea of the kind of word you need will do. It's often enough simply to predict whether the missing word is positive or negative.*

 DECIDE IN ADVANCE WHAT SORT OF WORD SHOULD FILL THE BLANK OR BLANKS.

3. Select the Best Match by Comparing Your Prediction with Each Answer Choice

 READ EVERY ANSWER CHOICE BEFORE DECIDING.

4. Read the Sentence with Your Answer Choice in the Blank or Blanks

If you've gone through the four steps and more than one choice seems possible, don't get stuck on the sentence. Eliminate whatever choices you can; guess; and move on. If a question really stumps you, circle it and come back when you're done with the section.

HINT: Only one choice will really make sense.

 REREAD THE SENTENCE WITH YOUR CHOICE PLUGGED IN.

Here's how the Four-Step Method works on some examples.

EXAMPLE A

Alligators, who bask in the sun for hours, appear to be - - - - creatures, yet they are quite capable of sudden movement.

(A) active

(B) violent

(C) stern

(D) content

(E) sluggish

1. Read the Sentence Carefully, Looking for Clue Words

Yet is a major clue. It tells you that the sentence switches direction midstream. The word in the blank must be something opposed to *sudden*.

2. Predict the Word That Goes in the Blank

You can guess that alligators seem like *lazy* or *idle* creatures.

3. Compare Your Prediction with Each Answer Choice, and Pick the Best Match

(A) *active* has nothing to do with being lazy or idle.

Neither does (B) *violent.*

Neither does (C) *stern.*

Neither does (D) *content.*

But (E), *sluggish,* means *inactive* or *slow moving,* so pick (E).

4. Check Your Answer by Plugging It Into the Sentence

Let's check: "Alligators, who bask in the sun for hours, appear to be sluggish creatures, yet they are quite capable of sudden movement." Sounds good. None of the other choices works in the sentence, so (E) is correct.

> HINT: *Try to avoid reading the sentence five times, plugging in every answer choice. That method takes too much time and should be used only if you're stuck. Instead, think about the question before you look for the answer.*

EXAMPLE B

The king's - - - - decisions as a diplomat and administrator led to his legendary reputation as a just and - - - - ruler.

(A) quick . . capricious

(B) equitable . . wise

(C) immoral . . perceptive

(D) generous . . witty

(E) clever . . uneducated

1. Read the Sentence Carefully, Looking for Clue Words

A big clue here is the phrase *led to*. You know that the kind of decisions the king made gave him a reputation as a just and - - - - ruler. So whatever goes in both blanks must be consistent with *just*.

2. Predict the Word that Goes in the Blank

Notice that both blanks must be similar in meaning. Because of his - - - - decisions, the king is viewed as a just and - - - - ruler. So if the king's decisions were good, he'd be remembered as a good ruler, and if his decisions were bad, he'd be remembered as a bad ruler. *Just*, which means "fair," is a positive-sounding word; you can predict that both blanks will be similar in meaning, and that both will be positive words. Write a "+" in the blanks or over the columns of answer choices to remind you.

3. Compare Your Prediction With Each Answer Choice, and Pick the Best Match

One way to do this is to determine which answers are both positive and similar.

In (A), *quick* and *capricious* aren't both positive and similar. (*Capricious* means "erratic or fickle.")

In (B), *equitable* means "fair." *Equitable* and *wise* are similar, and they're both positive. When you plug them in, they make sense, so (B) looks right. But check out the others to be sure.

In (C), *immoral* and *perceptive* aren't similar at all. *Perceptive* is positive but *immoral* isn't.

In (D), *generous* and *witty* are both positive adjectives, but they aren't really similar and they don't make sense in the sentence. Generous decisions would not give one a reputation as a witty ruler.

In (E), *clever* and *uneducated* aren't similar. *Clever* is positive, but *uneducated* isn't.

4. Check Your Answer by Plugging It Into the Sentence

"The king's equitable decisions as a diplomat and administrator led to his legendary reputation as a just and wise ruler." (B) makes sense in the sentence. So (B)'s our answer.

PICKING UP ON CLUES

To do well on Sentence Completions, you need to see how a sentence fits together. Clue words help you do that. The more clues you get, the clearer the sentence becomes, and the better you can predict what goes in the blanks.

What do we mean by *clue words*? Take a look at this example.

> Though some have derided it as - - - - , the search for
> extraterrestrial intelligence has actually become a
> respectable scientific endeavor.

Here, the word *though* is an important clue. *Though* contrasts the way some have derided, belittled, or ridiculed the search for extraterrestrial intelligence, with the fact that that search has become respectable. Another clue is *actually. Actually* completes the contrast: *Though* some see the search one way, it has *actually* become respectable.

You know that whatever goes in the blank must complete the contrast implied by the word *though.* So, to fill in the blank, you need a word that would be used to describe the opposite of "a respectable scientific endeavor." *Useless* or *trivial* would be a good prediction for the blank.

Try using clue words to predict the answers to the two questions below. First, look at the sentences without the answer choices and:

- Circle clue words.
- Think of a word or phrase that might go in each blank.
- Write your prediction below each sentence.

1. One striking aspect of Caribbean music is its - - - - of many African musical - - - - , such as call-and-response singing and polyrhythms.

2. Although Cézanne was inspired by the Impressionists, he - - - - their emphasis on the effects of light and - - - - an independent approach to painting that emphasized form.

Here are the same two questions with their answer choices (and with their clue words italicized). Now find the right answer to each question, referring to the predictions you just made.

1. One striking aspect of Caribbean music is its - - - - of many African musical - - - - , *such as* call-and-response singing and polyrhythms.

   (A) recruitment . . groups

   (B) proficiency . . events

   (C) expectation . . ideas

   (D) absorption . . forms

   (E) condescension . . priorities

2. *Although* Cézanne was inspired by the Impressionists, he - - - - their emphasis on the effects of light and - - - - an independent approach to painting that emphasized form.

   (A) accepted . . developed

   (B) rejected . . evolved

   (C) encouraged . . submerged

   (D dismissed . . aborted

   (E) nurtured . . founded

 CIRCLE CLUE WORDS.

By the way, the answers to the two questions above are (D) and (B). In question 1, *such as* tells you that the second blank must be something (genres, practices, forms) of which call-and-response singing and polyrhythms are examples. *Although* in question 2 tells you that the first blank must contrast with Cézanne's being "inspired" by the Impressionists.

Let's finish the day with a quiz to solidify what you've learned.

SENTENCE COMPLETIONS POP QUIZ

Answer 6 questions (4 minutes). Select the lettered word or set of words that best completes the sentence.

1. In the years following World War II, almost all Canadian Inuits - - - - their previously nomadic lifestyle; they now live in fixed settlements.

    (A) abandoned

    (B) continued

    (C) fashioned

    (D) preserved

    (E) rebuilt

2. A newborn infant's - - - - skills are not fully - - - - , for it cannot discern images more than 10 inches away.

   (A) perceptual . . stimulated

   (B) visual . . developed

   (C) descriptive . . ripened

   (D) olfactory . . shared

   (E) average . . familiar

3. Some geysers erupt regularly, while others do so - - - - .

   (A) consistently

   (B) copiously

   (C) perennially

   (D) sporadically

   (E) violently

4. Because of the lead actor's - - - - performance, the play received poor reviews from influential theater critics, and was canceled only one week after it opened.

   (A) erudite

   (B) corporeal

   (C) overwrought

   (D) fractious

   (E) resplendent

5. Sociologists have found that, paradoxically, many children of unorthodox, creative parents grow up to be rather tame - - - - .

   (A) idealists

   (B) conformists

   (C) individualists

   (D) alarmists

   (E) elitists

6. In Han mortuary art, the - - - - and the - - - - are combined; one tomb may contain eerie supernatural figures placed next to ordinary likenesses of government administrators at work.

   (A) fantastic . . mundane

   (B) inventive . . remorseful

   (C) illusory . . derivative

   (D) enlightened . . conservative

   (E) unique . . historical

EXPLANATIONS

1. (A)

The semicolon indicates that what follows—the statement that the Inuit now live in fixed settlements—is a continuation of the thought that came before. *Nomadic* means "wandering, transient," so, to be consistent, the first part of the sentence must say that the Inuit rejected, or abandoned, "their previously nomadic lifestyle."

2. (B)

For means "since" here, indicating that what follows is an explanation or clarification. What can be clarified by a statement that a newborn infant "cannot discern [perceive] images more than ten inches from its face"? The statement that the infant's ability to see things has not fully evolved. In other words, a newborn's visual skills are not fully developed. (In (D), *olfactory* means "relating to sense of smell.")

3. (D)

The clue words *while others* indicate contrast. If some geysers "erupt regularly," we can predict that these "others" do so irregularly. The best choice is (D): *sporadically* means "infrequently or irregularly."

4. (C)

The clue words *because of* signal an explanation. If the play "received poor reviews" and was canceled because of something about the lead actor's performance, that performance must have been quite bad. (C), overwrought—overdone, or excessively agitated—is one of two negative words in the answer choices, and the only one that could logically describe a performance (*fractious,* choice (D), means "cranky" or "cantankerous").

5. (B)

Paradoxically (or, in other words, "contrary to what one would expect"), children of creative and unorthodox parents grow up to be something other than creative and unorthodox. We need a word that contrasts with "creative and unorthodox" but goes along with *tame.* (B) is the best choice: Conformists are people who follow established norms and customs without challenging anything or anyone.

6. (A)

Again, a semicolon indicates a continuation of the same thought. If the statement that "one tomb contains eerie supernatural figures" and "ordinary likenesses of government administrators" is supposed to continue the first part of the sentence, then it must be true that Han mortuary art combines the unearthly or bizarre with the ordinary or everyday. The best answer is (A): In Han art, the fantastic (eerie supernatural figures) and the mundane (administrators) are combined.

STEP FOUR RECAP

- Use the Kaplan Four-Step Method for Sentence Completions:
    1. Read the sentence carefully.
    2. Predict the answer.
    3. Select the best match.
    4. Read the sentence with your answer choice in the blank or blanks.
- Clue words like *and, but, such as,* and *although* tell you how the parts of a sentence are related to each other.
- Decide in advance what sort of word should fill the blank or blanks.
- Read every answer choice before deciding.
- Reread the sentence with your choice plugged in.
- Circle clue words.

Step 5:
Critical Reading
Basic Techniques

If You Can Read This Message, You Can Succeed at Critical Reading

Improving your Critical Reading score means building skills you already have and applying them to the SAT. You don't need outside knowledge to answer the Critical Reading questions. And you don't need an amazing vocabulary, since unfamiliar terms will be defined for you. In fact, defining words from context is one of the things the SAT asks you to do—in Vocabulary-in-Context questions, which we'll cover in Step 6.

Critical Reading passages and questions are very predictable. You'll be given four reading passages, of 400 to 850 words each, drawn from the arts, humanities, social sciences, sciences, and fiction. One of these is a "paired passage" consisting of two related passages.

Most questions will ask about the overall tone and content of a passage, its details, and what it suggests. For paired passages, you'll also be asked to compare and contrast the related passages.

 STATISTIC: The 40 Critical Reading questions count for over half of your verbal score.

40 Critical Reading Questions

The Format

Critical Reading instructions are simple: "Answer questions based on what is stated or implied in the accompanying passage or passages." That's all the guidance the test makers give you. We'll give you more.

Each reading passage, first of all, begins with a brief introduction. Don't even think of skipping it.

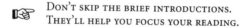

☞ DON'T SKIP THE BRIEF INTRODUCTIONS. THEY'LL HELP YOU FOCUS YOUR READING.

After the passage come the questions. Critical Reading questions have a specific order: The first few questions ask about the beginning of the passage, the last few about the end.

Questions following "paired passages" are also ordered: In general, the first few questions ask about the first passage, the next few about the second passage, and the final ones about the passages as a pair.

Unlike all other kinds of questions on the SAT, Critical Reading questions are not ordered by difficulty. On Critical Reading, the location of a question tells you nothing about its potential difficulty. So don't get bogged down on a hard Critical Reading question. The next one might be a lot easier.

As you'll see, certain kinds of Critical Reading questions— Vocabulary-in-Context questions, for instance—can often be done easily and quickly, even if you haven't read the passage. These are the questions to seek out if you're running out of time.

> HINT: Critical Reading questions are not ordered by
> difficulty.

Some people find Critical Reading passages dull or intimidating. While there is no way to jazz up a dry passage, you can try turning Critical Reading into a game.

Each passage is written for a purpose: The author wants to make a point, describe a situation, or convince you of his or her ideas. Sometimes, the little intro will tell you what the purpose is. Sometimes you must figure it out for yourself.

Recognize that every Critical Reading passage is made up of related paragraphs, and that each paragraph, in turn, is composed of a big idea and supporting details. As you read, you should always ask yourself, "What is the big idea of this paragraph? What are the details? How do the paragraphs work together?" Reading, while asking these kinds of questions, is called "Active Reading." It means reading lightly, but with a focus. You can practice Active Reading by identifying the big idea in the following paragraphs

PART TWO: Verbal

Identify the author's Big Idea in the following passages, using the accompanying hints.

1. The years between 1890 and 1940 marked the golden age of gardening in America. The wealthy knew no limit when it came to extravagance in their gardens. In the 1920s, one Massachusetts woman employed a hundred gardeners and caretakers, spending an annual $13,000 on flowers.

1. Big Idea: _____

Hint: $13,000 spent on flowers is a Detail.

2. The Alps appear to be victims of their own grandeur. It is tempting to overlook many of the area's environmental problems because their impact isn't immediately obvious; the Alps still seem magnificent in their matchless beauty. Beneath the stunning physical appearance of the region, however, a great deal of harm has already been done. In a strange twist of fate, this vast European mountain chain is being destroyed by the very tourists it attracts. For example, 20 million skiers visit the Alps every year. The Alpine roads are clogged by endless streams of vacationers in traffic jams 80 miles long.

2. Big Idea: _____

Hint: Can 20 million skiers be wrong?

Do you see how each of these paragraphs was composed of one big idea and supporting details? In the first paragraph, the big idea was contained in the first sentence: Gardening flourished between 1890 and 1940. The rest of the passage just supports this idea. In the second paragraph, the big idea is contained in the middle of the passage: The Alps are being destroyed by tourists.

As you read Critical Reading passages, you should look for the big idea and details the way you did with these two small paragraphs.

Now try the exercise below.

LOCATING THE DETAILS

Identify the author's Big Idea in the following passages, and give some examples of details.

3. During the first half of the twentieth century, many wine connoisseurs believed French wines to be superior to all others. All this changed in 1976, however, in what has come to be known as the Paris Tasting. That year, expert French wine critics blind-tasted several California wines alongside French wines. When the wines were revealed, the French critics were stunned to discover that they had awarded the top prize to the California wines over what many considered to be the best French wines of the time.

3. Big Idea: _____

Details: _____

_____

The big idea of the first paragraph is contained in the second sentence; after the wine tasting of 1976, French wines were no longer considered the best in the world. Details like *blind tasting* and *stunned to discover* support how California wines usurped the position of French wines.

4. The legend of Billy the Kid remains indelible in American lore. A folk hero of the old West, his authentic history is difficult to differentiate from the legend. The process of myth making had already set in a few months before the Kid's death, thanks to a ravenous hunger east of the 100th meridian for gory news of the rawboned west. Billy the Kid's mythological status was due as well to the florid prose and imaginations of the Western newspaper editors, who painted him as a "young demon" and "urged by a spirit hideous as hell." In the past, as they are today, Americans were eager to aggrandize the story of the young outlaw in an untamed land.

4. Big Idea: _____

Details: _____

_____

In the second paragraph, the big idea is found in the first sentence: Billy the Kid is a mythological hero in American lore. Phrases like *florid prose* and *ravenous hunger* are details that show how the Kid became a hero.

As you read through Critical Reading passages, you should try to uncover the big idea and details just as you have done with the small paragraphs above.

Try to read through the following passage. Don't be intimidated by its size; you have already read this much text in the exercise above. As you read the passage, identify the author's main point, and the big idea of the succeeding paragraphs. That way, you will have a "mental map" of the author's argument/point of view.

In this essay, the author writes about her childhood on a Caribbean island that was an English colony for many years.

When I saw England for the first time, I was a child in school
sitting at a desk. The England I was looking at was laid out on
a map gently, beautifully, delicately, a very special jewel; it lay
Line on a bed of sky blue, its yellow form mysterious, because
(5) though it looked like a leg of mutton,* it could not really look
like anything so familiar as a leg of mutton because it was
England. England was a special jewel all right, and only special
people got to wear it. The people who got to wear England
were English people. They wore it well and they wore it
(10) everywhere: in jungles, in deserts, on plains, in places where
they were not welcome, in places they should not have been.
When my teacher had pinned this map up on the blackboard,
she said, "This is England"—and she said it with authority,
seriousness, and adoration, and we all sat up. We understood
(15) then—we were meant to understand then—that England was
to be our source of myth and the source from which we got
our sense of reality, our sense of what was meaningful, our
sense of what was meaningless—and much about our own
lives and much about the very idea of us headed that last list.
(20) At the time I was a child sitting at my desk seeing England for
the first time, I was already very familiar with the greatness of
it. Each morning before I left for school, I ate a breakfast of
half a grapefruit, a bowl of oat porridge, bread and butter and
a slice of cheese, and a cup of cocoa. The can of cocoa was
(25) often left on the table in front of me. It had written on it the
name of the company, the year the company was established,
and the words "Made in England." Those words, "Made in
England," were written on the box the oats came in too. The
shoes I wore were made in England; so were my socks and
(30) cotton undergarments and the satin ribbons I wore tied at the
end of two plaits of my hair. My father, who might have sat
next to me at breakfast, was a carpenter and cabinet maker.
The shoes he wore to work would have been made in England,

as were his khaki shirt and trousers, his underpants and
(35) undershirt, his socks and brown felt hat. Felt was not the
proper material from which a hat that was expected to provide
shade from the hot sun should be made, but my father must
have seen and admired a picture of an Englishman wearing
such a hat in England. As we sat at breakfast a car might go
(40) by. The car, a Hillman or a Zephyr, was made in England. The
very conception of the meal itself, breakfast, and its
substantial quality and quantity was an idea from England; we
somehow knew that in England they began the day with this
meal called breakfast and a proper breakfast was a big
(45) breakfast.

At the time I saw this map—seeing England for the first
time—I did not say to myself, "Ah, so that's what it looks
like," because there was no longing in me to put a shape to
those three words that ran through every part of my life, no
(50) matter how small; for me to have had such a longing would
have meant that I lived in a certain atmosphere, an
atmosphere in which those three words were felt as a burden.
But I did not live in such an atmosphere. My father's brown
felt hat would develop a hole in its crown, the lining would
(55) separate from the hat itself, and six weeks before he thought
that he could not be seen wearing it—he was a very vain
man—he would order another hat from England. And my
mother taught me to eat my food in the English way: the knife
in the right hand, the fork in the left, my elbows held still close
(60) to my side. When I had finally mastered it, I overheard her
saying to a friend, "Did you see how nicely she can eat?" But I
knew then that I enjoyed my food more when I ate it with my
bare hands, and I continued to do so when she wasn't looking.
And when my teacher showed us the map, she asked us to
(65) study it carefully, because no test we would ever take would
be complete without this statement: "Draw a map of England."

I did not know then that the statement "Draw a map of
England" was something far worse than a declaration of war. I
did not know then that this statement was part of a process
(70) that would result in my erasure, not my physical erasure, but

my erasure all the same. I did not know then that this
statement was meant to make me feel in awe and small
whenever I heard the word "England": awe at its existence,
small because I was not from it. I did not know very much of
(75) anything then—certainly not what a blessing it was that I was
unable to draw a map of England correctly.

*the flesh of a sheep

How did you do? Yes, this was a tough passage. But you should have
gotten the general idea—that the author resents somewhat the
strong influence England had on every aspect of her childhood. As
the introduction told you, this island was "an English colony for
many years." It's clear throughout that the author rebels against her
"erasure"—that is, the assumption that she and her country were
insignificant compared to mighty England. So that's all you really
need to take away from a quick reading of the passage. Remember,
reading the passage won't earn you points—it's correctly answering
the questions that count.

STEP FIVE RECAP

- Don't skip the brief introductions. They'll help you focus
  your reading.
- Read the passage quickly, with a focus on its general
  outline.

STEP 6:
CRITICAL READING
FOCUSED TECHNIQUES

ALL CRITICAL READING QUESTIONS ARE NOT EQUAL

Most SAT Critical Reading questions fall into three basic types. Big Picture questions test your overall understanding of the passage's general outline. Little Picture questions ask about localized bits of information. Vocabulary-in-Context questions ask for the meaning of a single word.

> HINT: *Remember to skip around if you need to. You can tackle whichever passage you like in any order you like within the same section. But once you've read through the passage, try all the questions that go with it.*

BIG PICTURE QUESTIONS

Big Picture questions test your overall understanding of a passage. They might ask about:

- Main point or purpose of a passage
- Author's attitude or tone

- Logic underlying the author's argument
- How ideas relate to each other

One way to see the Big Picture is to read actively. As you read, ask yourself, "What's this all about? What's the point of this? Why is the author saying this?"

> HINT: Still stumped after reading the passage? Do the Little Picture questions first. They can help you fill in the Big Picture.

Turn back to the passage you tried in the previous step. What did you get out of the first reading? Something like "England was a profound influence on the author's early life, and she resents that"? That would have been enough.

Now look at question 5. It's a Big Picture question, asking for the main point of the passage. Use the Five-Step Method to find your answer.

5. The main purpose of the passage is to

   (A) advocate a change in the way a subject is taught in school

   (B) convey the personality of certain figures from the author's childhood

   (C) describe an overwhelming influence on the author's early life

   (D) analyze the importance of a sense of place to early education

   (E) relate a single formative episode in the author's life

1. Read the Question Stem

Simple enough: What's the main point of the passage?

2. Locate the Material You Need

In this case, you're asked about the overall point. You should have gotten a sense of that from reading the passage.

3. Get an Idea of the Right Answer

Again, you just need a rough statement. Here, something like this would do: "The purpose is to describe how England was a huge influence, and how the author resented that."

4. Scan the Answer Choices

(C) should have popped out. But (D) might also have looked good if you focused on the words "sense of place." So put those two aside as contenders. (A), how a subject was taught in school, is too narrow, and the same goes for (B), figures in the author's childhood, and (E), a single formative episode.

5. Select Your Answer

You've crossed off the poor choices, and you're down to two possibilities. Which matches your ideal? (C) comes closer. Look closely at (D) and you'll see that it's too general, too impersonal. Go with the best choice.

 DO BIG PICTURE QUESTIONS AFTER LITTLE PICTURE QUESTIONS IF YOU'RE NOT CLEAR ON THE MAIN IDEA OF THE PASSAGE.

LITTLE PICTURE QUESTIONS

More than two thirds of Critical Reading questions ask about Little Pictures. Little Picture questions usually refer you to a particular line or paragraph. That's a strong clue to where in the passage you'll find your answer.

Little Picture questions might:

- Test whether you understand significant information that's stated in the passage
- Ask you to make inferences or draw conclusions based on a part of the passage
- Ask you to relate parts of the passage to one another

Question 2 is a Little Picture question:

2. The author's reference to felt as "not the proper material" (lines 35–36) for her father's hat chiefly serves to emphasize her point about the

   (A) extremity of the local weather

   (B) arrogance of island laborers

   (C) informality of dress on the island

   (D) weakness of local industries

   (E) predominance of English culture

You're asked about the felt hat of the author's father; what does this point emphasize? Applying Kaplan's Step 2, locate the material you'll need. You're given a clue—a line reference—to help you here. Reread that, and the lines before and after it as well.

HINT: Don't pick farfetched inferences. SAT inferences tend to be strongly implied in the passage.

So why did the father wear a felt hat, which was probably quite hot in the tropical sun? Because it was English. That's what correct choice (E) says. Rereading that bit of the passage should have led you straight to that answer. (A) comes close, but doesn't fit the general thrust of the passage, which has little to do with describing the local weather but a lot to do with the overpowering influence of England. Even with Little Picture questions, grasping the general thrust of the passage can help you find the correct answer.

 MAKE SURE YOUR ANSWER TO A LITTLE PICTURE QUESTION MAKES SENSE IN THE CONTEXT OF THE PASSAGE.

Now try this question.

3. For the author, the requirement to "Draw a map of England" (line 66) represented an attempt to

   (A) force students to put their studies to practical use

   (B) glorify one culture at the expense of another

   (C) promote an understanding of world affairs

   (D) encourage students to value their own heritage

   (E) impart outmoded and inappropriate knowledge

The answer is (B).

VOCABULARY-IN-CONTEXT

Vocabulary-in-Context questions ask about an even smaller part of the passage than other Little Picture questions do; they ask about the usage of a single word. These questions do not test your ability to define hard words like "archipelago" and "garrulous." They do test your ability to infer the meaning of a word from context.

The words tested in these questions may be familiar to you; often they are fairly common words with more than one definition. Many of the answer choices will be definitions of the tested word, but only one will work in context. Vocabulary-in-Context questions always have a line reference, and you should always use it!

> HINT: Context is the most important part of Vocabulary-in-Context questions.

Sometimes one of the answer choices will jump out at you. It'll be the most common meaning of the word in question—but it's rarely right! We call this the "obvious" choice. For example, say *curious* is the word being tested. The obvious choice is "inquisitive." But *curious* also means "odd," and that's more likely to be the answer. Using context to find the answer will help prevent you from falling for this trap. You can use these choices to your advantage, though: If you get stuck on a Vocabulary-in-Context question, you can eliminate the "obvious" choice and take a guess instead.

 IF A VOCABULARY-IN-CONTEXT QUESTION HAS AN "OBVIOUS" CHOICE, BE WARY OF IT.

VOCABULARY-IN-CONTEXT PRACTICE

Here's some practice with Vocabulary-in-Context questions. Remember, don't just pick a common definition of the word in question. Pick the choice that defines what it means in context.

> The word *conception* as used in line 41 means
>
> (A) beginning
>
> (B) image
>
> (C) origination
>
> (D) notion
>
> (E) plan

> The word *erasure* (line 70) as used by the author most nearly means
>
> (A) total annihilation
>
> (B) physical disappearance
>
> (C) sense of insignificance
>
> (D) enforced censorship
>
> (E) loss of freedom

The answer to the first question is (D), and the answer to the second question is (C).

PAIRED PASSAGES—A (NOT SO) SPECIAL CASE

Don't let the paired passages worry you—they're not twice as hard as the single reading selections. With paired passages, you'll need to focus as you read on the relationship between the two passages. Just as with single passages, the questions following paired passages can help fill in the picture.

> IMPORTANT: Questions following paired passages are also ordered. In general, the first few questions relate to the first passage, the next few to the second passage, and the final questions ask about how the passages relate.

How to Do Paired Passages
1. Skim the first passage, looking for the general outline (as you would with a single passage).
2. Do the questions that relate to the first passage.
3. Skim the second passage, looking for the general outline and thinking about how the second passage relates to the first.
4. Do the questions that relate to the second passage.
5. Now you're ready to do the remaining questions, which will ask about the relationship between the two passages.

Alternating skimming passages and answering questions is especially important if you're short of time. You'll be able to answer at least some of the questions (and get a few extra points) before time runs out. By the time you've looked at both passages and answered the questions about each passage, you'll have a firm sense of the relationship between the pair. That will help you to answer the questions relating the two.

 TAKE THE PAIRED PASSAGES ONE AT A TIME.

WHAT TO DO IF YOU RUN OUT OF TIME

It's always best to skim the passage before you hit the questions. But if you only have a few minutes left, here's how to score points even while time is running out.

You can answer Vocabulary-in-Context questions and many Little Picture questions without reading the passage. If the question has a line reference, locate the material you need to find your answer and follow the Five-Step Method as usual. You won't have the overall picture to guide you, but you might be able to reach the correct answer just by understanding the "Little Picture."

 IF YOU'RE RUNNING OUT OF TIME, SKIP READING A PASSAGE AND JUST DO ITS VOCABULARY-IN-CONTEXT QUESTIONS FIRST, THEN ITS LITTLE PICTURE QUESTIONS.

CRITICAL READING POP QUIZ

Answer 7 questions (10 minutes). Questions 1–7 are based on the following passage.

The following excerpt is from a speech delivered in 1873 by Susan B. Anthony, a leader in the women's rights movement of the 19th century.

Friends and fellow-citizens: I stand before you tonight under indictment for the alleged crime of having voted at the last Presidential election, without having a lawful right to vote.

Line It shall be my work this evening to prove to you that in thus
(5) voting, I not only committed no crime, but, instead, simply exercised my citizen's rights, guaranteed to me and all United States citizens by the National Constitution, beyond the power of any State to deny.

The preamble of the Federal Constitution says:

(10) "We, the people of the United States, in order to form a more perfect union, establish justice, insure domestic tranquillity, provide for the common defense, promote the general welfare, and secure the blessings of liberty to ourselves and our posterity, do ordain and establish this

(15) Constitution for the United States of America."

It was we, the people; not we, the white male citizens; nor yet we, the male citizens; but we, the whole people, who formed the Union. And we formed it, not to give the blessings of liberty, but to secure them; not to the half of ourselves and

(20) the half of our posterity, but to the whole people—women as well as men. And it is a downright mockery to talk to women of their enjoyment of the blessings of liberty while they are denied the use of the only means of securing them provided by this democratic-republican government—the ballot.

(25) For any State to make sex a qualification that must ever result in the disfranchisement* of one entire half of the people

is a violation of the supreme law of the land. By it the blessings of liberty are forever withheld from women and their female posterity. To them this government had no just powers

(30) derived from the consent of the governed. To them this government is not a democracy. It is not a republic. It is an odious aristocracy; a hateful oligarchy of sex; this oligarchy of sex, which makes father, brothers, husband, sons, the oligarchs over the mother and sisters, the wife and daughters

(35) of every household—which ordains all men sovereigns, all women subjects, carries dissension, discord and rebellion into every home of the nation.

Webster, Worcester and Bouvier all define a citizen to be a person in the United States, entitled to vote and hold office.

(40) The one question left to be settled now is: Are women persons? And I hardly believe any of our opponents will have the hardihood to say they are not. Being persons, then, women are citizens; and no State has a right to make any law, or to enforce any old law, that shall abridge their privileges or

(45) immunities. Hence, every discrimination against women in the constitutions and laws of the several States is today null and void, precisely as is every one against Negroes.

*disfranchisement: deprivation of the right to vote.

1. In the first paragraph, Anthony states that her action in voting was

(A) illegal, but morally justified

(B) the result of her keen interest in national politics

(C) legal, if the Constitution is interpreted correctly

(D) an illustration of the need for a women's rights movement

(E) illegal, but worthy of leniency

Ⓐ Ⓑ Ⓒ Ⓓ Ⓔ

PART TWO: Verbal

2. By saying "we, the people . . ., the whole people, who formed the Union" (lines 16–18), Anthony means that

    (A) the founders of the nation conspired to deprive women of their rights

    (B) some male citizens are still being denied basic rights

    (C) the role of women in the founding of the nation is generally ignored

    (D) society is endangered when women are deprived of basic rights

    (E) all people deserve to enjoy the rights guaranteed by the Constitution

3. In the fourth paragraph (lines 25–37), Anthony's argument rests mainly on the strategy of convincing her audience that

    (A) any state that denies women the vote undermines its status as a democracy

    (B) women deprived of the vote will eventually raise a rebellion

    (C) the nation will remain an aristocracy if the status of women does not change

    (D) women's rights issues should be debated in every home

    (E) even an aristocracy cannot survive without the consent of the governed

KAPLAN

4. The word *hardihood* in (line 42) could best be replaced by

   (A) endurance

   (B) vitality

   (C) nerve

   (D) opportunity

   (E) stupidity

5. When Anthony warns that "no State . . . shall abridge their privileges" (lines 43–44), she means that

   (A) women should be allowed to live a life of privilege

   (B) women on trial cannot be forced to give up their immunity

   (C) every state should repeal its outdated laws

   (D) governments may not deprive citizens of their rights

   (E) the rights granted to women must be decided by the people, not the state

Explanations

1. (C)

This question is keyed to paragraph 1, where the second sentence gives you Anthony's declaration that she "not only committed no crime, but . . . simply exercised my citizen's rights, guaranteed me . . . by the National Constitution." Her act, in other words, was legal according to her reading of the Constitution. So (C) is correct.

2. (E)

Anthony points out here that no subgroup was excluded by the wording of the Constitution's "we, the people" preamble. That preamble refers "not to the half of ourselves . . . but to . . . women as well as men." So (E) is the best answer. (D) may have appealed to you, but it's wrong since it describes a claim that Anthony doesn't make until the following paragraph (note those line references!).

3. (A)

In the paragraph referred to, Anthony says that any state that prohibits women from voting violates federal law—the Constitution. A state that does so becomes "an odious aristocracy, a hateful oligarchy." In other words, a state that denies women the vote can't legitimately call itself either a democracy or a republic, so (A) is the best restatement of this rather subtle inference.

4. (C)

Hardihood is a strange word, but its meaning is clear in the keyed sentence. Anthony says, essentially, that her opponents wouldn't "have the hardihood" to claim that women are not persons. These opponents wouldn't, in other words, have the "nerve" to do so, choice (C). (Treat this like a Sentence Completion: Look for a word that could replace "hardihood" in the sentence; don't just look for any acceptable definition of *hardihood*.)

5. (D)

To *abridge* means to "curtail" or "decrease" in some way, so Anthony is arguing here that, since women are citizens, no state can curtail or decrease or deprive them of their rights. (D) is therefore the best answer.

STEP SIX RECAP

- Do Big Picture questions after Little Picture questions if you're not clear on the main idea of the passage.
- Make sure your answer to a Little Picture question makes sense in the context of the passage.
- If a Vocabulary-in-Context question has an "obvious" choice, be wary of it.
- Take the paired passages one at a time.
- If you're running out of time, skip reading a passage and do its Vocabulary-in-Context questions first, then its Little Picture questions.

PART THREE

MATH

STEP 7:
QC TECHNIQUES

QCs ARE A GIFT TO THOSE IN THE KNOW

In Quantitative Comparisons, instead of solving for a particular value, you need to compare two quantities. At first, QCs may appear really difficult because of their unfamiliar format. However, once you get used to them, they can be quicker and easier than the other types of Math questions, and a surefire way to pile up fast points.

> *STATISTIC: The 15 QCs count for one-fourth of your Math score.*

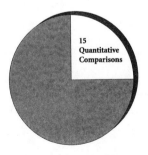

PART THREE: MATH

WHERE THEY APPEAR

The 15 QCs appear in the 30-minute Math section that also contains the ten Grid-in questions (you'll learn about those in Step 11). The QCs are arranged in order of increasing difficulty.

THE DIRECTIONS

The directions you'll see will look something like the following. Don't freak! We'll explain them in real English.

DIRECTIONS FOR QUANTITATIVE COMPARISON QUESTIONS

Compare the boxed quantity in Column A with the boxed quantity in Column B. Select answer choice.	**EXAMPLES**
A if Column A is greater	Column A Column B Answers
B if Column B is greater	
C if the columns are equal; or	**E1** 3×4 $3 + 4$ ⬤ⒷⒸⒹⒺ
D if more information is needed to determine the relationship	
An E response will be treated as an omission	x / $20°$
Notes:	
1 Some questions include information about one or both quantities. That information is centered and unboxed.	**E2** x $160°$ ⒶⒷ⬤ⒹⒺ
2 A symbol that appears in both Column A and Column B stands for the same thing in both columns.	x and y are positive
	E3 $x + 1$ $y - 1$ ⒶⒷⒸ⬤Ⓔ
3 All numbers used are real numbers	

   MEMORIZE WHAT THE QC ANSWER CHOICES
STAND FOR. KNOW THEM COLD BY TEST DAY.

As you've seen, the above directions can be intimidating. What they boil down to is this: In each question, you'll see two mathematical expressions, one in Column A, the other in Column B. Here's a sample (we'll explain this problem on page 95):

Column A	Column B
$x(x-1)$	$x^2 - x$

Some questions will include additional information about one or both of the quantities. This information will be centered above the two quantities.

Your job is to compare the quantities in each column. If Column A is bigger, choose (A); if Column B is bigger, choose (B); if they're equal, choose (C); and if you don't have enough information to tell, choose (D).

> *WARNING: Choice (E) is never the answer to a QC. Be careful not to mark (E) when you mean (D).*

 NEVER MARK CHOICE (E) ON A QC.

TWO RULES FOR ANSWER CHOICE (D)

Notice that choices (A), (B), and (C) all represent definite relationships between the quantities in Column A and Column B. But choice (D) represents a relationship that cannot be determined. Here are two things to remember about choice (D) that will help you decide when to pick it.

PART THREE: MATH

1. Choice (D) is never correct if both columns contain only numbers, without variables.

The relationship between numbers is unchanging and can always be established, but choice (D) means that more than one relationship is possible.

 NEVER PICK CHOICE (D) IF BOTH COLUMNS IN A QC CONTAIN ONLY NUMBERS (NO VARIABLES).

2. Choice (D) is correct if you can demonstrate two different relationships between the columns.

Suppose you ran across the following QC:

Column A	Column B
$2x$	$3x$

If x is a positive number, Column B is greater than Column A. If $x = 0$, the columns are equal. If x equals any negative number, Column B is less than Column A. Since more than one relationship is possible, (D) must be correct. In fact, as soon as you find a second possibility, stop work and pick choice (D).

 IF YOU CAN DEMONSTRATE TWO DIFFERENT RELATIONSHIPS BETWEEN THE COLUMNS, PICK CHOICE (D).

QC TOP TIPS

STRATEGY 1: COMPARE, DON'T CALCULATE

The key to QC success is not spending time on elaborate calculations. Remember that you're not looking for a specific answer here; you're just looking for the relative size of the two quantities. So, instead of calculating, compare the two quantities.

Here are four top Kaplan strategies that will enable you to make quick comparisons.

STRATEGY 2: MAKE ONE COLUMN LOOK LIKE THE OTHER

When the quantities in Columns A and B are expressed differently, you can often make the comparison easier by changing one column to look like the other. For example, if one column is a percent, and the other a fraction, try converting the fraction to a percent. Or, if the expression under Column A is in hours while that under Column B is in minutes, put the two on an equal footing by converting the figure in Column A to minutes.

Column A	Column B
$x(x-1)$	$x^2 - x$

Here Column A has parentheses, and Column B doesn't. So make Column A look more like Column B: Get rid of those parentheses. You end up with $x^2 - x$ in both columns, which means they are equal and the answer is (C).

Try another example, this one involving geometry.

Column A	Column B

The diameter of circle O is d and the area is a.

$$\frac{\pi d^2}{2} \qquad\qquad\qquad\qquad a$$

Make Column B look more like Column A by rewriting a, the area of the circle, in terms of the diameter, d. The area of any circle equals πr^2, where r is the radius.

Since the radius is half the diameter, we can plug in $\frac{d}{2}$ for r in the area formula to get $\pi\left(\frac{d}{2}\right)^2$ in Column B. Simplifying, we get $\frac{\pi d^2}{4}$.

Since both columns now contain πd^2 in the numerator, we can get rid of both and simply compare $\frac{1}{2}$ with $\frac{1}{4}$. Column A is greater, so the answer is choice (A).

☞ MAKE THE TERMS IN BOTH COLUMNS SIMILAR.

STRATEGY 3: DO THE SAME THING TO BOTH COLUMNS

Some QC questions become much clearer if you change not just the appearances, but the values of both columns. Treat them like two sides of an inequality, with the sign temporarily hidden.

You can add or subtract the same amount from both columns, and multiply or divide by the same positive amount without altering the relationship.

But watch out. Multiplying or dividing an inequality by a negative number reverses the direction of the inequality sign, as does squaring a fraction, so don't do it.

> *WARNING: Don't multiply or divide both QC columns*
> *by a negative number. Be careful with fractions.*
> *Remember that negative numbers and fractions behave*
> *very differently from positive integers!*

In the QC below, what could you do to both columns?

Column A		Column B
	$4a + 3 = 7b$	
$20a + 10$		$35b - 5$

All the terms in the two columns are multiples of 5, so divide both columns by 5 to simplify. You're left with $4a + 2$ in Column A and $7b - 1$ in Column B. This resembles the equation given in the centered information. In fact, if you add 1 to both columns, you have $4a + 3$ in Column A and $7b$ in Column B. The centered equation tells us they are equal. Thus choice (C) is correct.

In the next QC, what could you do to both columns?

Column A		Column B
	$y > 0$	
$1 + \dfrac{y}{(1 + y)}$		$1 + \dfrac{1}{(1 + y)}$

KAPLAN 97

Solution: First subtract 1 from both sides. That gives you $\dfrac{y}{(1+y)}$ in Column A, and $\dfrac{1}{(1+y)}$ in Column B. Get rid of the identical denominators and you're left comparing y with 1.

You know y is greater than 0, but it could be a fraction less than 1, so it could be greater or less than 1. Since you can't say for sure which column is greater, the answer is (D).

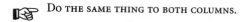 Do the same thing to both columns.

STRATEGY 4: PICK NUMBERS

If a QC involves variables, try picking numbers to make the relationship clearer. Here's what you do:

- Pick numbers that are easy to work with.
- Plug in the numbers and calculate the values. Note the relationship between the columns.
- Pick another number for each variable and calculate the values again. Is it the same relationship?

Column A	Column B
	$r > s > t > w > 0$	
$\dfrac{r}{t}$	$\dfrac{s}{w}$

Try $r = 4$, $s = 3$, $t = 2$, and $w = 1$. Then Column A $= \dfrac{r}{t} = \dfrac{4}{2} = 2$. And

Column B $= \dfrac{s}{w} = \dfrac{3}{1} = 3$. So in this case Column B is greater than

Column A.

Always Pick More Than One Number and Calculate Again

In the example above, we first found that Column B was bigger. But this doesn't mean that Column B is *always* bigger and that the answer is (B). It *does* mean that the answer is not (A) or (C). But the answer could still be (D), not enough information to decide.

If time is short here, guess between (B) and (D). But whenever you can, pick another set of numbers and calculate again.

Make a special effort to find a second set of numbers that will alter the relationship. Here for example, try making r a lot larger. Pick $r = 30$ and keep the other variables as they were. Now Column A $= \dfrac{30}{2} = 15$. This time, Column A is greater than Column B, so choice (D) is the correct answer.

> IMPORTANT: *If the relationship between Columns A and B changes when you pick other numbers, (D) must be the answer.*

Pick Different Kinds of Numbers

Don't assume that all variables represent positive integers. Unless you're told otherwise, variables can represent zero, negative numbers, or fractions. Since different kinds of numbers behave differently, always pick a different kind of number the second time around. In the example above, we plugged in a small positive number the first time and a larger number the second.

In the next three examples, we pick different numbers in the way outlined above. In which cases is the answer (D)?

Column A	Column B
w	$-w$

If $w = 5$, Column A = 5 and Column B = -5, so Column A is greater.

If $w = -5$, Column A = -5 and Column B = 5, so Column B is greater.

The relationship between the columns changes, so the answer is (D).

Column A	Column B

$$w \neq 0$$

Column A	Column B
w	$\dfrac{1}{w}$

If $w = 3$, Column A = 3 and Column B = $\dfrac{1}{3}$, so Column A is greater.

If $w = \dfrac{1}{3}$, Column A = $\dfrac{1}{3}$ and Column B = $\dfrac{1}{\frac{1}{3}}$ = 3, so Column B is

greater. Again, since the relationship changes depending on which numbers we pick, the answer is (D).

Column A	Column B
	$w > 1$
w	w^2

If $w = 1.1$, Column A $= 1.1$ and Column B $= 1.21$, so Column B is greater.

If $w = 70$, Column A $= 70$ and Column B $= 4,900$, so Column B is greater again. Here, we have not been able to demonstrate a changing relationship. The answer is B.

 PLUG IN TWO DIFFERENT SETS OF NUMBERS, AND COMPARE COLUMNS FOR EACH.

STRATEGY 5: AVOID COMMON QC TRAPS

To avoid QC traps, always be alert. Don't assume anything. Be especially cautious near the end of the question set.

Don't be tricked by misleading information.

Column A	Column B
John is taller than Bob.	
John's weight in pounds	Bob's weight in pounds

The test makers hope you'll think, "If John is taller, he must weigh more." But there's no guaranteed relationship between height and weight, so you don't have enough information. The answer is (D).

Don't Assume

A common QC mistake is to assume that variables represent positive integers. As we saw in using the number-picking strategy, fractions or negative numbers often show another relationship between the columns.

Column A	Column B
When 1 is added to the square of x the result is 37.	
x	6

It is easy to assume that x must be 6, since the square of x is 36. That would make choice (C) correct. However, it's possible that $x = -6$. Since x could be either 6 or -6, the answer is (D).

HINT: Be aware of negative numbers!

Don't Forget to Consider Other Possibilities

Column A	Column B
R	
S	
$+ T$	
$\overline{}$	
$1W$	

In the addition problem above, R, S, and T are different digits that are multiples of 3, and W is a digit.

Column A	Column B
W	8

Since you're told that R, S, and T are digits and different multiples of 3, most people will think of 3, 6, and 9, which add up to 18. That makes W equal to 8, and Columns A and B equal. But that's too obvious for a QC at the end of the section.

There's another possibility: 0 is also a digit and a multiple of 3. So the three digits could be 0, 3, and 9, or 0, 6, and 9, which give totals of 12 and 15, respectively. That means W could be 8, 2, or 5. Since the columns could be equal, or Column B could be greater, answer choice (D) must be correct.

Don't Fall for Look-Alikes

Column A	Column B
$\sqrt{5} + \sqrt{5}$	$\sqrt{10}$

At first glance, forgetting the rules of radicals, you might think that these quantities are equal and the answer is (C). But use some common sense to see this isn't the case. $\sqrt{5}$ has to be bigger than $\sqrt{4}$ (which is 2), so $\sqrt{5} + \sqrt{5}$ in Column A has to be bigger than 4. Meanwhile, $\sqrt{10}$ in Column B is *smaller* than another familiar number, $\sqrt{16}$, so Column B is less than 4. The answer is (A).

 DON'T ASSUME THAT ALL VARIABLES ARE POSITIVE NUMBERS, OR THAT NUMBERS THAT LOOK ALIKE, ARE ALIKE.

Now that you've got a handle on QCs, finish off today's lesson with the following Pop Quiz.

QC Pop Quiz

Answer 7 questions (6 minutes). Choose (A) if Column A is greater; (B) if Column B is greater; (C) if the columns are equal; or (D) if more information is needed to determine the relationship.

	<u>Column A</u>		<u>Column B</u>

$$x = 2y$$
$$y > 0$$

1. 4^{2y} 2^x

Ⓐ Ⓑ Ⓒ Ⓓ Ⓔ

q, r, and s are positive integers

$$qrs > 12$$

2. $\dfrac{qr}{5}$ $\dfrac{3}{s}$

Ⓐ Ⓑ Ⓒ Ⓓ Ⓔ

$$\frac{x}{y} = \frac{z}{4}$$

x, y, and z are positive

3. $6x$ $2yz$

Ⓐ Ⓑ Ⓒ Ⓓ Ⓔ

$$x > 1$$
$$y > 0$$

4. y^x $y^{(x+1)}$

Ⓐ Ⓑ Ⓒ Ⓓ Ⓔ

$$h > 1$$

5. The number of minutes in *h* hours

    $$\frac{60}{h}$$

Ⓐ Ⓑ Ⓒ Ⓓ Ⓔ

$$7p + 3 = r$$
$$3p + 7 = s$$

6. *r*   *s*

Ⓐ Ⓑ Ⓒ Ⓓ Ⓔ

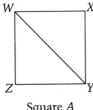

Square *A*   Square *B*

Note: Figures not drawn to scale.

7. $$\frac{\text{Perimeter of square } A}{\text{Perimeter of square } B}$$

    $$\frac{\text{Length of } WY}{\text{Length of } PR}$$

Ⓐ Ⓑ Ⓒ Ⓓ Ⓔ

Explanations

1. (A)

Replacing the x exponent in Column B with the equivalent value given in the problem, we're comparing 4^{2y} to 2^{2y}. Since $y > 0$, raising 4 to the $2y$ power yields a greater value than raising 2 to the $2y$ power.

2. (D)

Do the same thing to both columns to make them look like the centered information. When we multiply both sides by $5s$ we get qrs in Column A and 15 in Column B. Since qrs could be any integer greater than 12, it could be greater than, equal to, or less than 15.

3. (B)

Do the same thing to both columns until they resemble the centered information. When we divide both columns by $6y$ we get $\dfrac{6x}{6y}$, or $\dfrac{x}{y}$ in Column A, and $\dfrac{2yz}{6y}$, or $\dfrac{z}{3}$ in Column B. Since $\dfrac{x}{y} = \dfrac{z}{4}$, and $\dfrac{z}{3} > \dfrac{z}{4}$ (because z is positive), $\dfrac{z}{3} > \dfrac{x}{y}$.

4. (D)

Pick numbers. Try $x = y = 2$. Then Column A $= yx = (2)(2) = 4$. Column B $= y^{x+1} = 2^3 = 8$, making Column B greater. But if $x = 2$

and $y = \dfrac{1}{2}$ Column A = $\left(\dfrac{1}{2}\right)^2 = \dfrac{1}{4}$ and Column B = $\left(\dfrac{1}{2}\right)^3 = \dfrac{1}{8}$.

In this case, Column A is greater than Column B, so the answer is (D).

5. (A)

It's a trap! The "obvious" answer here is choice (C), because there are 60 minutes in an hour, and 60 appears in Column B. But the number of minutes in h hours would equal 60 times h, not 60 divided by h. Try picking numbers: If h is 2 (it has to be greater than 1), the number in Column A would be 60(2) or 120. The number in Column B would be $\dfrac{60}{2}$, or 30. Column A is greater, and that holds even if you pick a much larger number for h. (A) is correct.

6. (D)

Pick a value for p, and see what effect this has on r and s. If $p = 1$, $r = (7 \times 1) + 3 = 10$, and $s = (3 \times 1) + 7 = 10$, and the two columns are equal. But if $p = 0$, $r = (7 \times 0) + 3 = 3$, and $s = (3 \times 0) + 7 = 7$, and Column A is smaller than Column B. Since there are at least two different possible relationships, the answer is choice (D).

7. (C)

We don't know the exact relationship between Square A and Square B, but it doesn't matter. The problem is actually just comparing the ratios of corresponding parts of two squares. Whatever the relationship between them is for one specific length in both squares, the same relationship will exist between them for any other corresponding length. If a side of one square is twice the length of a side of the second square, the diagonal will also be twice as long. The ratio of the perimeters of the two squares is the same as the ratio of the sides. Therefore, the columns are equal. (C) is correct.

STEP SEVEN RECAP

- Memorize what the QC answer choices stand for. Know them cold by Test Day.
- Never mark choice (E) on a QC.
- Never pick choice (D) if both columns in a QC contain only numbers (no variables).
- If you can demonstrate two different relationships between the columns, choose choice (D).
- Use Kaplan's Top Four QC Strategies:
    1. Make the terms in both columns similar.
    2. Do the same thing to both columns.
    3. Plug in two different sets of numbers, and compare columns for each.
    4. Avoid traps. Don't assume that all variables are positive numbers, or that numbers that look alike, are alike.

STEP 8: CALCULATOR TECHNIQUES

YOUR CALCULATOR IS NOT ALWAYS YOUR FRIEND

You are allowed to use a calculator on the SAT. That's a mixed blessing. The good news is that you can do computation faster. The bad news is that you may be tempted to waste time using a calculator on questions that shouldn't involve lengthy computation.

Remember, you never *need* a calculator to solve an SAT problem. If you ever find yourself doing extensive calculation—elaborate division or long drawn-out multiplication—stop and look again, because you probably missed a shortcut.

SHOULD I BRING A CALCULATOR?

You definitely will want to bring your calculator on Test Day. By zeroing in on the parts of problems that need calculation, you can increase your score and save yourself time on the SAT by using your calculator.

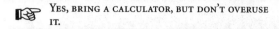 YES, BRING A CALCULATOR, BUT DON'T OVERUSE IT.

WHAT KIND OF CALCULATOR SHOULD I BRING?

The best calculator to bring is one you're comfortable with. The most important thing is not how fancy your calculator is, but how good you are at using it. *If you don't have a calculator now, buy one right away, and practice using it between now and Test Day.* Remember that you won't be doing logs, trig functions, or preprogrammed formulas on the SAT.

You can use just about any small calculator except:

- Calculators that print out your calculations
- Handheld minicomputers or laptop computers
- Any calculators with a typewriter keypad
- Calculators with an angled readout screen
- Calculators that require an external power supply

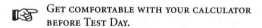 GET COMFORTABLE WITH YOUR CALCULATOR BEFORE TEST DAY.

WHEN SHOULD I USE A CALCULATOR?

Calculators help the most on Grid-ins and the least on QCs.

The reason for this is that QCs are designed to be done very quickly, and never involve much computation; if you think you need a calculator on them, you're missing something. Both Grid-ins and Regular Math will sometimes involve computation—never as the most important part of the question, but often as a final step.

Since Grid-ins, as we'll see, don't give you answer choices to choose from, it's especially important to be sure of your work. Calculators can help you check your work and avoid careless errors.

Remember, a calculator can be useful when used selectively and strategically. Not all parts of a problem will necessarily be easier with a calculator. Consider this problem:

> If four grams of cadmium yellow pigment can make 3 kilograms of cadmium yellow oil paint, how many kilograms of paint could be produced from 86 grams of pigment?

This word problem has two steps. Step one is to set up the following proportion:

$$\frac{4 \text{ gm}}{3 \text{kg}} = \frac{86 \text{ gm}}{x \text{ kg}}$$

A little algebraic engineering tells you that:

$$x \text{ kg} = \frac{3 \text{ kg} \times 86 \text{ gm}}{4 \text{ gm}}$$

Here's where you whip out that calculator. This problem has now been reduced down to pure calculation: $(3 \times 86) \div 4 = 64.5$.

PART THREE: Math

WHEN SHOULDN'T I USE A CALCULATOR?

Don't be fooled. On most SAT problems you may be tempted to use your calculator, but many questions will be easier without it. That's particularly true of QCs.

Consider this problem:

Column A	Column B
$\dfrac{5}{8} + \dfrac{8}{15}$	$\dfrac{4}{9} + \dfrac{10}{21}$

Sure, you could grab your calculator and divide out those fractions. You could then calculate the two sums and compare the columns. But why bother?

If you just compare these terms to $\dfrac{1}{2}$ you'll be out of this problem much faster. After all, $\dfrac{5}{8}$ and $\dfrac{8}{15}$ from column A are both greater than $\dfrac{1}{2}$, and $\dfrac{4}{9}$ and $\dfrac{10}{21}$ (from column B) are both less than $\dfrac{1}{2}$. Quantity A must be greater.

Using your calculator would have slowed you down.

Be careful on non-QC questions, too. Consider this:

If $x^2 \times 8^2 = 49 \times 64 \times 81$, $x^2 =$

    (A) 49^2

    (B) 56^2

    (C) 63^2

    (D) 72^2

    (E) 81^2

Now if you punch in $49 \times 64 \times 81$ you'll get 254,016. But that won't be too helpful. Look at the answer choices! Instead, realize that:

$$(x^2) \times 8^2 = (49 \times 81) \times 64.$$

8^2 is the same thing as 64, so get rid of the 64s on both sides. You get:

$$x^2 = 49 \times 81.$$

So that's $x^2 = 7^2 \times 9^2$ or $x^2 = 7 \times 7 \times 9 \times 9$ which is 63×63 or 63^2.

No calculator required.

 DON'T LET YOUR CALCULATOR BLIND YOU TO THE FAST SOLUTION TO A QUESTION.

TWO COMMON CALCULATOR MISTAKES

CALCULATOR MISTAKE #1: CALCULATING BEFORE YOU THINK

On the Grid-in problem below, how should (and shouldn't) you use your calculator?

> The sum of all the integers from 1 to 44, inclusive, is subtracted from the sum of all the integers from 7 to 50, inclusive. What is the result?

The Wrong Approach:

- Grab calculator.
- Punch in all the numbers.
- Put down answer and hope you didn't hit any wrong buttons.

Faced with this problem, you might be tempted to punch in all the numbers from 1 to 44, find their sum, then do the same for the numbers 7 through 50, and subtract the first sum from the second. But doing that means punching 252 keys. The odds are you'll slip up somewhere, hit the wrong key, and get the wrong answer. Even if you don't, punching in all those numbers takes too much time.

The Kaplan Approach:

- Think first.
- Decide on the best way to solve the problem.
- Only then, use your calculator.

The right approach is to think first. The amount of computation involved in directly solving this tells you that there must be an easier way. You'll see this if you realize that both sums contain the same number of consecutive integers. Each integer in the first sum has a corresponding integer 6 greater than it in the second sum:

1	7
+2	+8
+3	+9
.	.
.	.
.	.
+42	+48
+43	+49
+44	+50
=	=

How many pairs of integers are there? As we'll see in the Math Traps step, the way to find the number of integers in a consecutive series is to subtract the smallest from the largest and add 1 (44 − 1 = 43; 43 + 1 = 44 OR 50 − 7 = 43; 43 + 1 = 44) So there are 44 pairs of integers that are 6 apart.

Therefore, the total difference between the two sums will be the difference between each pair of integers times the number of pairs.

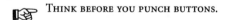 THINK BEFORE YOU PUNCH BUTTONS.

Now take out your calculator, punch "6 × 44 =," and get the correct answer of 264, with little or no time wasted.

> *WARNING: If you're punching buttons for long stretches*
> *at a time, you're approaching the problem the wrong way.*

CALCULATOR MISTAKE #2: FORGETTING THE ORDER OF OPERATIONS

Watch out. Even when you use your calculator, you can't just enter numbers in the order they appear on the page—you've got to follow the order of operations. This is a very simple error, but it can cost you lots of points. The order of operations is "PEMDAS," which stands for:

Parentheses

Exponents

Multiplication

Division

Addition

Subtraction

That means you do whatever is in parentheses first, then deal with exponents, then multiplication and division (from left to right), and finally addition and subtraction (from left to right).

For example, say you want to find the value of the expression $\dfrac{x^2 + 1}{x + 3}$ when $x = 7$.

If you just punched in "$7 \times 7 + 1 \div 7 + 3 =$" you would get the wrong answer.

The correct way to work it out is

$(7^2 + 1) \div (7 + 3) = (7 \times 7 + 1) \div (7 + 3) = (49 + 1) \div 10 = 50 \div 10 = 5$

 Remember PEMDAS (the order of operations) when making calculations. And make sure you know how your calculator handles multistep calculations.

Combining a calculator with an understanding of when and how to use it can help you boost your score.

Step Eight Recap

- Yes, bring a calculator, but don't overuse it.
- Get comfortable with your calculator *before* Test Day.
- Don't let your calculator blind you to the fast solution to a question.
- Think before you punch buttons.
- Remember PEMDAS (the order of operations) when making calculations. And make sure you know how your calculator handles multi-step calculations.

Step 9: Classic Math Techniques

At the start of each Math section you will find the following info:

Time—30 Minutes 25 Questions	Solve each of the following problems, decide which is the best answer choice, and darken the corresponding oval on the answer sheet. Use available space in the test booklet for scratchwork.

Notes:

(1) Calculator use is permitted.

(2) All numbers used are real numbers.

(3) Figures are provided for some problems. All figures are drawn to scale and lie in a plane UNLESS otherwise indicated.

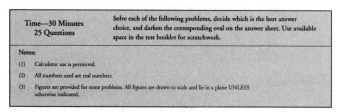

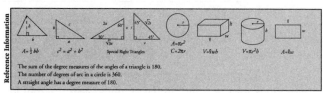

$A = \frac{1}{2} bh$ $c^2 = a^2 + b^2$ Special Right Triangles $A = \pi r^2$ $C = 2\pi r$ $V = lwh$ $V = \pi r^2 h$ $A = lw$

The sum of the degree measures of the angles of a triangle is 180.
The number of degrees of arc in a circle is 360.
A straight angle has a degree measure of 180.

- Note (2) means you won't have to deal with imaginary numbers, like *i* (the square root of –1).
- Note (3) tells you diagrams are drawn to scale (unless otherwise noted), which means you can use these diagrams to estimate measurements. However, if a diagram is labeled "Figure not drawn to scale," you can't do this.

- Note (3)'s reference to figures that "lie in a plane" simply means that you are dealing with flat figures, like rectangles or circles, unless the question says otherwise.
- The math information you're given includes many basic geometry formulas. By Test Day you should know all of these formulas. But if you find yourself drawing a blank on Test Day, it's nice to know that the formulas are spelled out in the directions.
- The QCs and Grid-ins have different instructions, which we'll discuss in detail later.

 LEARN THE MATH DIRECTIONS NOW SO THAT YOU DON'T EVEN HAVE TO LOOK AT THEM ON TEST DAY.

HOW TO APPROACH SAT MATH

To maximize your Math score, you need to use your time efficiently. Then you won't get bogged down on a single hard question and miss other problems you could have solved if you'd had more time.

The key to working systematically is to think about the question before you look for the answer. A few seconds spent up front looking for traps, thinking about your approach, and deciding whether to tackle the problem now or come back to it later will pay off in SAT points. On easy problems, you may know what to do right away. But on hard problems, the few extra seconds are time well spent.

THE KAPLAN SYSTEMATIC APPROACH TO MATH QUESTIONS

Let's see how you might use a systematic approach to the problem below:

12. At a certain diner, Joe orders 3 doughnuts and a cup of coffee and is charged $2.25. Stella orders 2 doughnuts and a cup of coffee and is charged $1.70. What is the price of 2 doughnuts?

(A) $0.55

(B) $0.60

(C) $1.10

(D) $1.30

(E) $1.80

1. Assess the Question's Difficulty

All SAT Math questions are arranged in order of difficulty. Within a set, the first questions are easy, the middle ones moderately difficult, and the last ones are hard. Problem #12 should be a moderately difficult word problem.

2. Read Through the Question Carefully

If you try to start solving the problem before reading it all the way through, you may end up doing unnecessary work.

HINT: On difficult questions, watch out for Math Traps. Hard questions are often designed to trip up careless readers. (For more on Math Traps, see Step 10.)

Make sure you know what's being asked. Problem #12 looks straightforward, but read through it carefully and you'll see a slight twist. You're asked to find the cost of *two* doughnuts, not one. Many people will find the price of a single donut and forget to double it. That's why this problem is #12 and not #2: There's a twist to it.

3. Decide Whether to Do the Problem or Skip It for Now

If you have no idea what to do, skip the problem. Spend your time on the problems you can solve.

If you think you can solve it, but it will take a lot of time, circle the question number in your test booklet and make a note to come back to it later if you have time.

If you can eliminate one or more answer choices, do so. Make an educated guess. In your test booklet, make a note to remind yourself that you guessed, and try solving the problem later if time permits. (For details on educated guessing, see Step 12.)

4. If You Do Tackle the Problem, Look for the Fastest Approach

Look for hidden information. On an easy question all the information you need to solve the problem may be given up front, in the stem, or in a diagram. But in a harder question, you may need to look for hidden information. Also, extraneous information may be thrown into the problem to get you off track. Since questions are arranged in order of difficulty, you should be a little wary of #12. If you got the answer too easily, you may have missed something. In this case, you're asked to find the price of two doughnuts, not one.

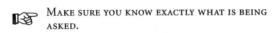 MAKE SURE YOU KNOW EXACTLY WHAT IS BEING
ASKED.

Look for shortcuts. Sometimes the obvious way of doing a problem is the long way. If the method you choose involves lots of calculating, look for another route. There's usually more than one way to solve a problem, and one of those ways won't involve you in tons of arithmetic. In problem #12, for example, the cost of doughnuts and coffee could be translated into two distinct equations using the variables d (for *doughnut*) and c (for *coffee*). You could find c in terms of d, then plug this in to the other equation. But if you think carefully, you'll see there's a quicker way: The difference in price between 3 doughnuts and a cup of coffee and 2 doughnuts and a cup of coffee is the price of 1 donut. So one doughnut costs $2.25 − $1.70 = $0.55. (Remember, you have to find the price of 2 doughnuts. Twice $0.55 is $1.10.)

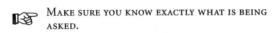 LOOK FOR SHORTCUTS.

Use a variety of strategies. The Math chapters of this book will review many strategies for specific problem types that will help you get to the answer faster.

5. If You Get Stuck, Make an Educated Guess

If you're not sure what to do, or if you tried solving a problem but got stuck, cut your losses. Eliminate whatever choices you can, and then guess. Since the Math choices are typically arranged in increasing or decreasing order, it's often easy to find and eliminate choices that are way too high or low.

> *HINT: When you skip a question, circle it or make a note in your test booklet to come back to it later, if you have time.*

Let's say it's taking too long to solve the donut problem. Can you eliminate any answer choices? The price of two doughnuts and a cup of coffee is $1.70. That means the cost of two doughnuts alone can't be $1.80, which eliminates choice (E). Now you can choose between the remaining choices, and your odds of guessing correctly have improved.

 IF YOU GET STUCK, MAKE AN EDUCATED GUESS.

If you practice using this Five-Step Systematic Approach to the Math problems on the SAT, you will save time and avoid mistakes on Test Day.

 USE THE KAPLAN SYSTEMATIC APPROACH TO MATH QUESTIONS.

SOME MORE MATH YOU KNEW BUT PROBABLY FORGOT

There are certain types of math skills that are tested again and again on the SAT. You almost certainly learned these skills in your math classes over the years, but are they still as sharp as they should be?

What you don't want to do is spend valuable time on Test Day dredging your memory for techniques you were taught years ago. Now is the time to sharpen up those rusty skills. In this step, we'll give you a quick brush-up on some of the SAT makers' favorite Math question types, along with Kaplan's classic pointers for solving them. These are by no means exhaustive discussions, but they should be enough to clear away a few mental cobwebs.

STATISTIC: The 35 Regular Math questions count for just over one-half of your Math score.

35 Regular Math Questions

The following techniques work for all SAT Math questions, whether Regular Math, QC, or Grid-in.

REMAINDERS

Remainder questions can be easier than they look. You might think you have to solve for a certain value, but often you don't. For example:

> When n is divided by 7, the remainder is 4. What is the remainder when $2n$ is divided by 7?
>
> (A) 0
>
> (B) 1
>
> (C) 2
>
> (D) 3
>
> (E) 4

The question above doesn't depend on knowing the value of n. In fact, n has an infinite number of possible values.

> *HINT: The easy way to solve this kind of problem is to pick a number for n.*

Which number should you pick? Since the remainder when n is divided by 7 is 4, pick any multiple of 7 and add 4. The easiest multiple to work with is 7. So, $7 + 4 = 11$. Use 11 for n.

Plug 11 into the question and see what happens:

- What is the remainder when $2n$ is divided by 7?
    the remainder when $2(11)$ is divided by 7?
    the remainder when 22 is divided by 7?
    $\dfrac{22}{7} = 3$ remainder 1

The remainder is 1 when $n = 11$. So the answer is (B). The remainder will also be 1 when $n = 18$, 25, or 46.

☞ PLUG IN NUMBERS WHEN SOLVING REMAINDER
QUESTIONS.

AVERAGES

Give this averages question a shot.

> The average weight of 5 dogs in a certain kennel is 32
> pounds. If 4 of the dogs weigh 25, 27, 19, and 35
> pounds, what is the weight of the fifth dog?
>
> (A) 28
>
> (B) 32
>
> (C) 49
>
> (D) 54
>
> (E) 69

Instead of giving you a list of values to plug into the average formula, SAT average questions often put a slight spin on the problem.
They tell you the average of a group of terms and ask you to find the
value of a missing term.

HINT: Work with the sum.

Let x = the weight of the fifth dog. Plug this into the average for formula, which is:

$$\text{Average} = \frac{\text{Sum of Terms}}{\text{Number of Terms}}$$

$$32 = \frac{25 + 27 + 19 + 35 + x}{5}$$

$$32 \times 5 = 25 + 27 + 19 + 35 + x$$

So the average weight of the dogs, times the number of dogs, equals the total weight of the dogs. The new formula is: Average × Number of Terms = Sum of Terms.

Remember this manipulation of the average formula so that, whenever you know the average of a group of terms and the number of terms, you can find the total sum.

Now you can solve for the weight of the fifth dog:

$$32 \times 5 = 25 + 27 + 19 + 35 + x$$
$$160 = 106 + x$$
$$54 = x$$

So the weight of the fifth dog is 54 pounds, choice (D).

☞ REMEMBER THAT AVERAGE × NUMBER OF TERMS = SUM OF TERMS.

RATIOS

Here's a ratio question:

Out of every 50 chips produced in a certain factory, 20 are defective. What is the ratio of nondefective chips produced to defective chips produced?

(A) 2:5

(B) 3:5

(C) 2:3

(D) 3:2

(E) 5:2

The key here is that the test makers try to get you to set up the wrong ratio.

HINT: Identify the parts and the whole in the problem.

Find the parts and the whole in the problem. In this case the total number of chips is the whole, and the number of nondefective chips and the number of defective chips are the parts that make up this whole.

You're given a part-to-whole ratio (the ratio of defective chips to all chips) and asked to find a part-to-part ratio (the ratio of nondefective chips to defective chips).

If 20 chips out of every 50 are defective, the remaining 30 chips must be nondefective. So the part-to-part ratio of nondefective to defective chips is $\frac{30}{20}$, or $\frac{3}{2}$, which is equivalent to 3:2, answer choice (D).

If you hadn't identified the part and the whole first it would be easy to get confused and compare a part to the whole, like the ratios in answer choices (A), (B), and (E).

This approach also works for ratio questions where you need to find actual quantities. Here's an example.

Out of every 5 chips produced in a certain factory, 2 are defective. If 2,200 chips were produced, how many were defective?

Here you need to find a quantity, the number of defective chips.

> *HINT: If you're looking for the actual quantities in a ratio, set up and solve a proportion.*

You're given a part-to-whole ratio (the ratio of defective chips to all chips), and the total of chips produced. You can find the answer by setting up and solving a proportion:

$$\frac{\text{Number of defective chips}}{\text{Total number of chips}} = \frac{2}{5} = \frac{x}{2{,}200}$$

x = number of defective chips

$$5x = 4{,}400 \text{ (by cross multiplying } \frac{2}{5} = \frac{x}{2{,}200} \text{)}$$

$$x = 880 \text{ (by dividing both sides by 5)}$$

> *HINT: Remember that ratios compare only relative size; they don't tell you the actual quantities involved.*

 DISTINGUISH CLEARLY BETWEEN THE PARTS AND THE WHOLE IN RATIO PROBLEMS.

RATES

Ready for a rate question?

> If 8 oranges cost a dollars, b oranges would cost how many dollars?
>
> (A) $8ab$
>
> (B) $\dfrac{8a}{b}$
>
> (C) $\dfrac{8}{ab}$
>
> (D) $\dfrac{a}{8b}$
>
> (E) $\dfrac{ab}{8}$

A *rate* is a ratio that compares quantities measured in different units. In the problem above, the units are dollars and oranges.

What makes this rate problem difficult is the presence of variables. It's hard to get a clear picture of the relationship between the units.

> HINT: *Pick numbers for the variables to make the relationship between the units clearer.*

Pick numbers for a and b that will be easy for you to work with in the problem.

Let $a = 16$. Then 8 oranges cost $16. So the cost per orange at this rate $= \dfrac{\$16}{8 \text{ oranges}} = \$2$ per orange.

Let $b = 5$. So the cost of 5 oranges at this rate is 5 oranges $\times$ \$2 per orange = \$10.

Now plug in $a = 16$ and $b = 5$ into the answer choices to see which one gives you a value of 10.

Choice (A): $8 \times 16 \times 5 = 640$. Eliminate.

Choice (B): $\dfrac{8 \times 16}{5} = \dfrac{128}{5}$. Eliminate.

Choice (C): $\dfrac{8}{16 \times 5} = \dfrac{1}{10}$. Eliminate.

Choice (D): $\dfrac{16}{8 \times 5} = \dfrac{2}{5}$. Eliminate.

Choice (E): $\dfrac{16 \times 5}{8} = 10$.

Since (E) is the only one that gives the correct value, it is correct.

☞ MAKE RATES PROBLEMS CONCRETE BY PLUGGING IN NUMBERS FOR VARIABLES.

PERCENTS

Now it's time for you to play the percentages.

> Last year Julie's annual salary was \$20,000. This year's raise brings her to an annual salary of \$25,000. If she gets a raise of the same percentage every year, what will her salary be next year?

(A) $27,500

(B) $30,000

(C) $31,250

(D) $32,500

(E) $35,000

In percent problems, you're usually given two pieces of information and asked to find the third. When you see a percent problem, remember the following formulas.

- If you are solving for a percent:

$$\text{Percent} = \frac{\text{Part}}{\text{Whole}}$$

- If you need to solve for a part:

$$\text{Percent} \times \text{Whole} = \text{Part}$$

This problem asks for Julie's projected salary for next year—that is, her current salary plus her next raise.

You know last year's salary ($20,000) and you know this year's salary ($25,000), so you can find the difference between the two salaries:

$25,000 − $20,000 = $5,000 = her raise

Now find the percent this raise represents by using the formula

$$\text{Percent} = \frac{\text{Part}}{\text{Whole}}.$$

Since Julie's raise was calculated on last year's salary, divide by $20,000.

> *HINT: Be sure you know which whole to plug in. Here you're looking for a percentage of $20,000, not of $25,000.*

$$\text{Percent} = \frac{\$5,000}{\$20,000} = \frac{1}{4} = 25\%$$

You know Julie will get the same percent raise next year, so solve for the part. Use the formula Percent × Whole = Part.

Her raise next year will be 25% × $25,000 = $\frac{1}{4}$ × 25,000 = $6,250.

Add that amount to this year's salary and you have her projected salary:

$25,000 + $6,250 = $31,250, or answer choice (C).

Make sure you change the percent to either a fraction or a decimal before beginning calculations.

☞ REMEMBER THAT PERCENT × WHOLE = PART.

SIMULTANEOUS EQUATIONS

If $p + 2q = 14$ and $3p + q = 12$, then $p =$

(Note: This is a Grid-in, so there are no answer choices.)

In order to get a numerical value for each variable, you need as many different equations as there are variables to solve for. So, if you have two variables, you need two distinct equations.

You could tackle this problem by solving for one variable in terms of the other, and then plugging this expression into the other equation. But the simultaneous equations that appear on the SAT can usually be handled in an easier way.

> HINT: *Combine the equations—by adding or subtracting them—to cancel out all but one of the variables.*

You can't eliminate p or q by adding or subtracting the equations in their present forms.

But if you multiply the second equation by 2:

$2(3p + q) = 2(12)$

$6p + 2q = 24$

Now when you subtract the first equation from the second, the qs will cancel out so you can solve for p:

$$6p + 2q = 24$$
$$-[p + 2q = 14]$$
$$\overline{}$$
$$5p + 0 = 10$$

If $5p = 10$, $p = 2$. On the answer sheet, you would grid in the answer 2.

ADD AND SUBTRACT SIMULTANEOUS EQUATIONS
TO CANCEL OUT VARIABLES.

SYMBOLISM

If $a \star b = \sqrt{a + b}$ for all non-negative numbers, what is
the value of $10 \star 6$?

(A) 0

(B) 2

(C) 4

(D) 8

(E) 16

You should be quite familiar with the arithmetic symbols +, −, ×,
and ÷. Finding the value of $10 + 2$, $18 − 4$, $4\ 3\ 9$, or $96 ÷ 16$ is easy.

However, on the SAT, you may come across bizarre symbols. You
may even be asked to find the value of $10 \star 2$, $5 ✿ 7$, $10 ✪ 6$, or
$65 ♦ 2$.

The test makers put strange symbols in questions to confuse or
unnerve you. Don't let them. The question stem always tells you
what the strange symbol means. Although this type of question may
look difficult, it is really just an exercise in plugging in.

To solve, just plug in 10 for a and 6 for b into the expression
$\sqrt{a + b}$ That equals $\sqrt{10 + 6}$, or $\sqrt{16}$ or 4: choice (C).

 DON'T FREAK OUT. JUST PLUG IN NUMBERS FOR
SYMBOLISM QUESTIONS.

SPECIAL TRIANGLES

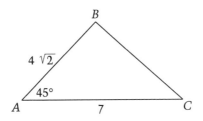

In the triangle above, what is the length of side *BC* ?

    (A) 4

    (B) 5

    (C) $4\sqrt{2}$

    (D) 6

    (E) $5\sqrt{2}$

> *HINT: Look for the special triangles in geometry problems.*

Special triangles contain a lot of information. For instance, if you know the length of one side of a 30-60-90 triangle, you can easily work out the lengths of the others. Special triangles allow you to transfer one piece of information around the whole figure.

The following are the special triangles you should look for on the SAT. You don't have to memorize the ratios (they're listed in the instructions), but you should be familiar enough with them to recognize them when you see them.

Equilateral Triangles

All interior angles are 60° and all sides have equal length.

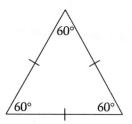

Isosceles Triangles

Two sides have equal length, and the angles facing these sides are equal.

Right Triangles

These contain a 90° angle. The sides are related by the Pythagorean theorem: $a^2 + b^2 = c^2$ where a and b are the legs and c is the hypotenuse.

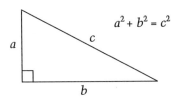

The "Special" Right Triangles

Many triangle problems contain "special" right triangles, whose side lengths always come in predefined ratios. If you recognize them, you won't have to use the Pythagorean theorem to find the value of a missing side length.

The 3-4-5 Right Triangle

(Be on the lookout for multiples of 3-4-5 as well.)

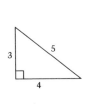
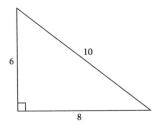

The Isosceles Right Triangle

(Note the side ratio: 1 to 1 to $\sqrt{2}$.)

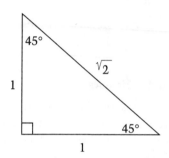

The 30-60-90 Right Triangle

(Note the side ratio: 1 to $\sqrt{3}$ to 2, and which side is opposite which angle.)

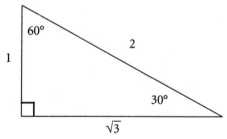

Getting back to our example, you can drop a vertical line from *B* to line *AC*. This divides the triangle into two right triangles.

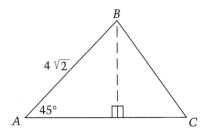

That means you know two of the angles in the triangle on the left: 90° and 45°. The third angle must also be 45°, so this is an isosceles right triangle, with sides in the ratio of 1 to 1 to $\sqrt{2}$. The hypotenuse here is $4\sqrt{2}$, so both legs have length 4. Filling this in, you have the following.

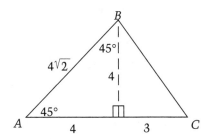

Now you can see that the legs of the smaller triangle on the right must be 4 and 3, making this a 3-4-5 right triangle, and the length of hypotenuse BC is 5. So choice (B) is correct.

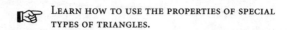

LEARN HOW TO USE THE PROPERTIES OF SPECIAL
TYPES OF TRIANGLES.

STEP NINE RECAP

- Learn the Math directions now so that you don't even have to look at them on Test Day.
- If you get stuck, make an educated guess.
- Use the Kaplan Five-Step Systematic Approach to Math Questions:
    1. Assess Difficulty.
    2. Read Question Carefully.
    3. Decide to Do or Skip.
    4. Look for Fastest Approach.
    5. If Stuck, Make an Educated Guess.
- Plug in numbers when solving remainder questions.
- Remember that Average × Number of Terms = Sum of Terms.
- Distinguish clearly between the parts and the whole in ratio problems.
- Make rates problems concrete by plugging in numbers for variables.
- Remember that Percent × Whole = Part.
- Add and subtract simultaneous equations to cancel out variables.
- Just plug in numbers for symbolism questions.

STEP 10:
MATH TRAP TECHNIQUES

LOOK BEFORE YOU LEAP

It's time for us to let you in on a little secret that will allow you to breeze through the entire SAT, get into any college you want, succeed in life, and find eternal happiness.

If you believed a word of the preceding sentence, you need to pay special attention to this chapter. This step presents eight common SAT traps. Traps lure you into one answer, usually an answer that's easy to get to. But they conceal the correct answer, which requires some thought. If you're not wary of traps on the SAT, they may trip you up. Learn to recognize common traps and you'll gain more points on Test Day.

HOW MATH TRAPS WORK AND HOW TO AVOID THEM

The same traps occur again and again on the SAT. You can boost your score by learning how they work and how to avoid them. Once you can deal with traps, you'll do much better on the harder math questions.

PART THREE: Math

Let's look at the eight most common math traps on the SAT.

TRAP #1: PERCENT INCREASE/DECREASE

Jackie purchased a new car in 1990. Three years later she sold it to a dealer for 40 percent less than she paid for it in 1990. The dealer then added 20 percent onto the price he paid and resold it to another customer. The price the final customer paid for the car was what percent of the original price Jackie paid in 1990?

(A) 40%

(B) 60%

(C) 72%

(D) 80%

(E) 88%

The Wrong Answer

The increase/decrease percentage problem usually appears at the end of a section and invariably contains a trap. Most students will figure that taking away 40 percent, and then adding 20 percent gives you an overall loss of 20 percent, and pick choice (D), 80 percent, as the correct answer. Wrong!

The Trap

When a quantity is increased or decreased by a percentage more than once, you cannot simply add and subtract the percents to get the answer.

In this kind of percent problem, the first percent change is a percent of the starting amount, but the second change is a percent of the *new* amount.

Avoiding the Trap

Percents can only be added and subtracted when they are percents of the same amount.

 DON'T BLINDLY ADD AND SUBTRACT PERCENTS.

Finding the Right Answer

We know:

- "40 percent less" that Jackie got for the car is 40 percent of her original price
- 20 percent the dealer adds on is 20 percent of what the dealer paid, a much smaller amount
- Adding on 20 percent of that smaller amount is not the same thing as adding back 20 percent of the original price

Solving the Problem Fast

Use 100 for a starting quantity, whether or not it's plausible in the real situation. The problem asks for the relative amount of change. So you can take any starting number, and compare it with the final result. Because you're dealing with percents, 100 is the easiest number to work with.

> *HINT: Pick 100 as the starting quantity.*

- If Jackie paid $100 for the car, what is 40 percent less?

In the case of $100, each percent equals $1, so $100 - 40 = 60$. Jackie sold the car for $60.

- If the dealer charges 20 percent more than his purchase price, he's raising the price by 20 percent of $60, which is $60 \times .20 = \$12$ (not 20 percent of $100, which would be $20!).
- Therefore, the dealer sold the car again for $60 + $12, or $72.
- Finally, what percent of the starting price ($100) is $72?
  $$\frac{72}{100} = 72\%.$$ So the correct answer here is choice (C).

TRAP #2: WEIGHTED AVERAGES

In a class of 27 students, the average (arithmetic mean) score of the boys on the final exam was 83. If the average score of the 15 girls in the class was 92, what was the average of the whole class?

(A) 86.2

(B) 87.0

(C) 87.5

(D) 88.0

(E) 88.2

The Wrong Answer

Some students will rush in and simply average 83 and 92 to come up with 87.5 as the class average.

The Trap

You cannot combine averages of different quantities by taking the average of those averages.

In an averages problem, if one value occurs more frequently than others it is "weighted" more. Remember that the average formula calls for the sum of all the terms, divided by the total number of terms.

Avoiding the Trap

Work with the sums, not the averages.

 DON'T JUST TAKE THE AVERAGE OF THE AVERAGES.

Finding the Right Answer

If 15 of the 27 students are girls, the remaining 12 must be boys.

We can't just add 83 to 92 and divide by two. In this class there are more girls than boys, and therefore the girls' test scores are "weighted" more—they contribute more to the class average. So the answer must be either (D) or (E). To find each sum, multiply each average by the number of terms it represents. After you have found the sums of the different terms, find the combined average by plugging them into the average formula.

$$\text{Total class average} = \frac{\text{Sum of girls' scores} + \text{sum of boys' scores}}{\text{Total number of students}}$$

$$= \frac{(\text{\# of girls 3 girls' average score}) + (\text{\# of boys 3 boys' average score})}{\text{Total number of students}}$$

$$= \frac{15(92) + 12(83)}{27} = \frac{1380+996}{27} = 88$$

So the class average is 88, answer choice (D). (Notice how using a calculator helps in this situation!)

TRAP #3: RATIO:RATIO:RATIO

> Mike's coin collection consists of quarters, dimes, and nickels. If the ratio of the number of quarters to the number of dimes is 5 to 2, and the ratio of the number of dimes to the number of nickels is 3 to 4, what is the ratio of the number of quarters to the number of nickels?
>
> (A) 5 to 4
> (B) 7 to 5
> (C) 10 to 6
> (D) 12 to 7
> (E) 15 to 8

The Wrong Answer

If you chose 5 to 4 as the correct answer, you fell for the classic ratio trap.

The Trap

Parts of different ratios don't always refer to the same whole.

In the classic ratio trap, two different ratios each share a common part that is represented by two different numbers. The two ratios do not refer to the same whole, however, so they are not in proportion to each other. To solve this type of problem, restate both ratios so that the numbers representing the common part (in this case "dimes") are the same. Then all the parts will be in proportion and can be compared to each other.

Avoiding the Trap

Make sure the common quantity in both ratios has the same number in both.

 RESTATE RATIOS SO THAT THE SAME NUMBER REFERS TO THE SAME QUANTITY.

Finding the Right Answer

To find the ratio of quarters to nickels, restate both ratios so that the number of dimes is the same in both.

We are given two ratios:

Quarters to Dimes = 5 to 2   Dimes to Nickels = 3 to 4

The number corresponding to dimes in the first ratio is 2. The number corresponding to dimes in the second ratio is 3. To restate the ratios, find the least common multiple of 2 and 3. The least common multiple of 2 and 3 is 2×3, or 6.

Restate the ratios with the number of dimes as 6:

Quarters to Dimes = 15 to 6 (which is the same as 5 to 2)
Dimes to Nickels = 6 to 8 (which is the same as 3 to 4)

The ratios are still in their original proportions, but now they can be compared easily, since dimes are represented by the same number in both.

The ratio of quarters to dimes to nickels is 15 to 6 to 8, so the ratio of quarters to nickels is 15 to 8, which is answer choice (E).

TRAP #4: UNSPECIFIED ORDER

Column A	Column B

A, B, and C are points on a line such that point A is 12 units away from point B and point B is 4 units away from point C.

The distance from point *A* to point *C*	16

The Wrong Answer

In problems about distances on a line, you should always draw a diagram to help you visualize the relationship between the points.

In this diagram, the distance from *A* to *C* is 16, which is the same as Column B. But choice (C)—the columns are not equal—is not the right answer.

The Trap

Don't assume that there is only one possible arrangement of the points. In this case, there's no reason to believe that the points lie in alphabetical order.

We are not told what the relationship between A and C is. In fact, C could lie to the left of B, as in the following diagram.

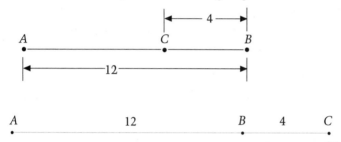

Avoiding the Trap

Don't assume points lie in the order they are given or in alphabetical order—look for alternatives.

 DON'T ASSUME THAT THERE IS ONLY ONE WAY TO DRAW A DIAGRAM.

Finding the Right Answer

In this second case, the distance from A to C is 8, which is less than Column B. Since we have two possible relationships between the columns, the answer must be (D)—you can't be certain from the data given.

TRAP #5: LENGTH:AREA RATIO

Column A	Column B
The area of a square with a perimeter of 14	Twice the area of a square with a perimeter of 7

The Wrong Answer

Twice the perimeter doesn't mean twice the area. Choice (C)—the columns are equal—is wrong.

The Trap

In proportional figures, the ratio of the areas is not the same as the ratio of the lengths.

Avoiding the Trap

Understand that the ratio of the areas of proportional figures is the square of the ratio of corresponding linear measures.

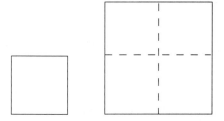

REMEMBER THAT IN PROPORTIONAL FIGURES,
THE RATIO OF AREAS IS NOT THE SAME AS THE
RATIO OF LENGTHS.

FINDING THE RIGHT ANSWER

One way to solve this QC would be to actually compute the respective areas.

A square of perimeter 14 has side length $\dfrac{14}{4}$ = 3.5. Its area then is $(3.5)^2 = 12.25$. On the other hand, the area of the square in Column B is $\left(\dfrac{7}{4}\right)^2 = (1.75)^2 = 3.0625$. Even twice that area is still less than the 12.25 in Column A. The answer is (A).

But this method takes too much time. A quicker and cleverer way to dodge this trap is to understand the relationship between the linear ratio and the area ratio of proportional figures. In proportional figures, the area ratio is the square of the linear ratio.

In the example above, we are given two squares with sides in a ratio of 14:7 or 2:1.

Using the rule above, we square the linear 2:1 ratio. The areas of the two figures will be in a 4:1 ratio.

The same goes for circles:

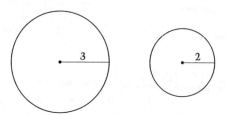

In the figure above, we are given two circles with radii in a 3:2 ratio. Using the rule above, we square the linear 3:2 ratio to get $3^2:2^2$, or 9:4. The areas of the two circles will be in a 9:4 ratio.

TRAP #6: HIDDEN INSTRUCTIONS

> At a certain restaurant, the hourly wage for a waiter is 20 percent greater than the hourly wage for a dishwasher, and the hourly wage for a dishwasher is half as much as the hourly wage for a cook's assistant. If a cook's assistant earns $8.50 an hour, how much less than a cook's assistant does a waiter earn each hour?
>
> (A) $2.55
>
> (B) $3.40
>
> (C) $4.25
>
> (D) $5.10
>
> (E) $5.95

The Wrong Answer

To solve this problem, you must find the hourly wage of the waiter.

- The cook's assistant earns $8.50 an hour.
- The dishwasher earns half that, or $4.25 an hour.

- The waiter earns 20 percent more than this: $4.25 × 1.2 = $5.10.
- So the waiter earns $5.10 an hour, and you might reach automatically to fill in answer choice (D). But (D) is the wrong answer.

The Trap

A small step, easily overlooked, can mean the difference between a right and wrong answer.

In this case the word is *less*. After spending all this time finding the waiter's hourly wage, many students skip right over the vital last step. They overlook the fact that the question asks not what the waiter earns, but how much less than the cook's assistant the waiter earns.

Avoiding the Trap

Make sure you answer the question that's being asked.

 WATCH FOR HIDDEN INSTRUCTIONS.

Finding the Right Answer

- You have figured out that the waiter earns $5.10 an hour.
- And the cook's assistant earns $8.50 an hour.
- To find out how much less than the cook's assistant the waiter earns, subtract the waiter's hourly wage from the cook's assistant's hourly wage.
- The correct answer is (B), $3.40.

TRAP #7: AVERAGE RATE

A car traveled from A to B at an average rate of 40 miles per hour and then immediately traveled back from B to A at an average speed of 60 miles per hour. What was the car's average speed for the round trip, in miles per hour?

(A) 45

(B) 48

(C) 50

(D) 52

(E) 54

The Wrong Answer

Do you see which answer choice is too "obvious" to be correct? The temptation is simply to average 40 and 60. The answer is "obviously" (C), 50. But 50 is wrong.

The Trap

To get an average rate, you can't just average the rates.

Why is the average speed not 50 mph? Because the car spent more time traveling at 40 mph than at 60 mph. Each leg of the round trip was the same distance, but the first leg, at the slower speed, took more time.

Avoiding the Trap

You can solve almost any Average Rate problem if you apply this general formula:

$$\text{Average Rate} = \frac{\text{Total Distance}}{\text{Total Time}}$$

Use the given information to figure out the Total Distance and the Total Time. But how can you do that when many problems don't specify the distances?

Finding the Right Answer

In our sample above, we are told that a car went "from A to B at 40 miles per hour and back from B to A at 60 miles per hour."

In other words, it went half the Total Distance at 40 mph and half the Total Distance at 60 mph.

How do you use the formula, $\text{Average Rate} = \frac{\text{Total Time}}{\text{Total Distance}}$, if you don't know the Total Distance?

> HINT: *Pick any number you want for the Total Distance.*
> *Pick a useful number!*

Divide that Total Distance into Half Distances

Calculate the time needed to travel each Half Distance at the different rates.

 WHEN PLUGGING NUMBERS INTO THE AVERAGE RATE FORMULA, PICK NUMBERS THAT ARE EASY TO WORK WITH.

A good number to pick here would be 240 miles for the Total Distance, because you can easily figure in your head the times for two 120-mile legs at 40 mph and 60 mph:

A to B: $\dfrac{120 \text{ miles}}{40 \text{ miles per hour}} = 3 \text{ hours}$

B to A: $\dfrac{120 \text{ miles}}{60 \text{ miles per hour}} = 2 \text{ hours}$

Total Time = 5 hours

"Total Distance = 240 miles," so "Total Time = 5 hours" can be plugged into the general formula:

$$\text{Average Rate} = \dfrac{\text{Total Distance}}{\text{Total Time}}$$

$$= \dfrac{240 \text{ miles}}{5 \text{ hours}}$$

$$= 48 \text{ miles per hour.}$$

Correct answer choice: (B).

TRAP #8: COUNTING NUMBERS

The tickets for a certain raffle are consecutively numbered. If Louis sold the tickets numbered from 75 to 148 inclusive, how many raffle tickets did he sell?

(Note: This is a Grid-in, so there are no answer choices.)

The Wrong Answer

Many people would subtract 75 from 148 to get 73 as their answer. But that is not correct.

The Trap

Subtracting the first and last integers in a range will give you the difference of the two numbers. It won't give you the number of integers in that range.

Avoiding the Trap

To count the number of integers in a range, subtract the endpoints and then add 1.

If you forget the rule, pick two small numbers that are close together, such as 1 and 4. Obviously, there are four integers from 1 to 4, inclusive. But if you had subtracted 1 from 4, you would have gotten 3. In the diagram below, you can see that 3 is actually the distance between the integers, if the integers were on a number line or a ruler.

 TO COUNT THE NUMBER OF INTEGERS IN AN INCLUSIVE RANGE, SUBTRACT THE ENDPOINTS AND THEN ADD 1.

Finding the Right Answer

In the problem above, subtract 75 from 148.

The result is 73.

Add 1 to this difference to get the number of integers.

That gives you 74. This is the number you would grid in on your answer sheet.

The word "inclusive" tells you to include the first and last numbers given. So "the integers from 5 to 15 inclusive" include 5 and 15. Questions always make it clear whether you should include the outer numbers or not, since the correct answer hinges on this point.

MATH TRAPS POP QUIZ

Answer 13 questions (10 minutes).

<u>Column A</u>   <u>Column B</u>

A car traveled the first half of a 100-kilometer distance at an average speed of 120 kilometers per hour and it traveled the remaining distance at an average speed of 80 kilometers per hour.

1. The car's average speed   100
    in kilometers per hour, for
    the 100 kilometers

Ⓐ Ⓑ Ⓒ Ⓓ Ⓔ

---

2. The ratio of $\frac{1}{4}$ to $\frac{2}{5}$ is equal to the ratio of $\frac{2}{3}$ to x.

    x $\frac{3}{5}$

Ⓐ Ⓑ Ⓒ Ⓓ Ⓔ

John buys 34 books at $6 each, and 17 at $12 each.

3. The average price John $9.00
    pays per book

Ⓐ Ⓑ Ⓒ Ⓓ Ⓔ

PART THREE: Math

<table>
<tr><td>Column A</td><td>Column B</td></tr>
</table>

On a certain highway, Town X lies 50 miles away from Town Y, and Town Z lies 80 miles from Town X.

4. The number of minutes a car traveling at an average speed of 60 miles per hour takes to travel from Town Y to Town Z

    30

    Ⓐ Ⓑ Ⓒ Ⓓ Ⓔ

5. The area of a circle with a diameter of 3

    The sum of the areas of 3 circles each with a diameter of 1

    Ⓐ Ⓑ Ⓒ Ⓓ Ⓔ

Jane invests her savings in a fund that adds 10 percent interest to her savings at the end of every year.

6. The percent by which her money has increased after 3 years

    31 percent

    Ⓐ Ⓑ Ⓒ Ⓓ Ⓔ

7. Pump 1 can drain a 400-gallon water tank in 1.2 hours. Pump 2 can drain the same tank in 1.8 hours. How many minutes longer than pump 1 would it take pump 2 to drain a 100-gallon tank?

    (A) 0.15

    (B) 1.2

    (C) 6

    (D) 9

    (E) 18

8. Volumes 12 through 30 of a certain encyclopedia are located on the bottom shelf of a bookcase. If the volumes of the encyclopedia are numbered consecutively, how many volumes of the encyclopedia are on the bottom shelf?

    (A) 17

    (B) 18

    (C) 19

    (D) 29

    (E) 30

PART THREE: Math

9. A reservoir is at full capacity at the beginning of summer. By the first day of fall, the level in the reservoir Is 30 percent below full capacity. Then during the fall a period of heavy rains raises the level by 30 percent. After the rains, the reservoir is at what percent of its full capacity?

    (A) 100%

    (B) 95%

    (C) 91%

    (D) 85%

    (E) 60%

10. Two classes, one with 50 students, the other with 30, take the same exam. The combined average of both classes is 84.5. If the larger class averages 80, what is the average of the smaller class?

    (A) 87.2

    (B) 89.0

    (C) 92.0

    (D) 93.3

    (E) 94.5

11. In a pet shop, the ratio of puppies to kittens is 7:6 and the ratio of kittens to guinea pigs is 5:3. What is the ratio of puppies to guinea pigs?

    (A) 7:3

    (B) 6:5

    (C) 13:8

    (D) 21:11

    (E) 35:18

---

12. A typist typed the first *n* pages of a book, where *n* > 0, at an average rate of 12 pages per hour and typed the remaining *n* pages at an average rate of 20 pages per hour. What was the typist's average rate, in pages per hour, for the entire book?

    (A) $14\frac{2}{3}$

    (B) 15

    (C) 16

    (D) 17

    (E) 18

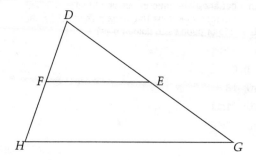

13. In triangle *DGH* above, *DE = EG, EF* ‖ *GH*, and the area of triangle *DGH* is 30. What is the area of triangle *DEF*?

    Answer: _____

(Note: This is a Grid-in question. In the actual SAT, you would write your answer in boxes and grid in the ovals beneath.)

EXPLANATIONS

How did you do? Did you spot the trap in each problem? Use the answers below to see what your weaknesses are. Each wrong answer represents one trap you need to work on. Go back and reread the section on that trap. Then try the problems again, until you answer right.

1. (B)
Average rates trap (see Trap #7, earlier in this step)

2. (A)
A variation on the Ratio:Ratio:Ratio trap—(see Trap #3)

3. (B)
Weighted averages trap (see Trap #2)

4. (D)
Unspecified order trap (see Trap #4)

5. (A)
Length:area ratio trap (see Trap #5)

6. (A)
Percent increase/decrease trap (see Trap #1)

7. (D)
Hidden instructions trap (see Trap #6)

8. (C)
Counting numbers trap (see Trap #8)

9. (C)
Percent increase/decrease trap (see Trap #1)

10. (C)
Weighted averages trap (see Trap #2)

11. (E)
Ratio:ratio:ratio trap (see Trap #3)

12. (B)
Average rates trap (see Trap #7)

13. 7.5
Length:area ratio trap (see Trap #5)

STEP TEN RECAP

- If you see what appears to be an easy problem late in a question set, there is probably a trap.
- Don't blindly add and subtract percents.
- Don't just take the averages of averages.
- Restate ratios so that the same number refers to the same quantity.
- Don't assume that there is only one way to draw a diagram.
- Remember that, in proportional figures, the ratio of the areas is not the same as the ratio of the lengths.
- Watch for hidden instructions.
- When plugging numbers into the Average Rate formula, pick numbers that are easy to work with.
- To count the numbers of integers in an inclusive range, subtract the endpoints and then add 1.

Step 11: Grid-in Techniques

Not Your Average SAT Question

In high school math class, you usually don't get five answer choices to pick from on a test. And you don't lose a quarter of a point for a wrong answer. Instead, you must simply find the answer to a problem.

The Grid-in section on the SAT is a lot like the math tests you're used to. Unlike other SAT Math questions, Grid-ins have no multiple-choice answers and there's no penalty for wrong answers. You have to figure out your own answer and fill it in on a special grid. Note that some Grid-ins have only one correct answer, while others have several correct credited answers, or even a range of such answers.

STATISTIC: The 10 Grid-ins count for one-sixth of your Math score.

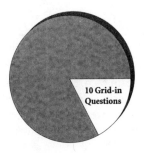

10 Grid-in Questions

PART FOUR: Putting It All Together

THE FORMAT

You'll get 10 Grid-ins, following the QCs, in one of the Math sections. Here's what the directions will look like.

DIRECTIONS FOR STUDENT-PRODUCED RESPONSE QUESTIONS

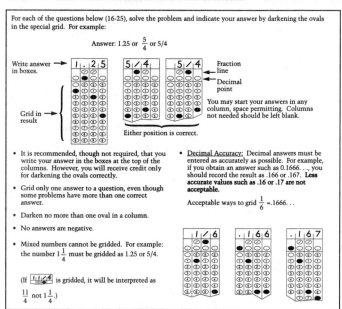

For each of the questions below (16-25), solve the problem and indicate your answer by darkening the ovals in the special grid. For example:

Answer: 1.25 or $\frac{5}{4}$ or 5/4

Write answer in boxes.

Grid in result

Either position is correct.

Fraction line

Decimal point

You may start your answers in any column, space permitting. Columns not needed should be left blank.

- It is recommended, though not required, that you write your answer in the boxes at the top of the columns. However, you will receive credit only for darkening the ovals correctly.

- Grid only one answer to a question, even though some problems have more than one correct answer.

- Darken no more than one oval in a column.

- No answers are negative.

- Mixed numbers cannot be gridded. For example: the number $1\frac{1}{4}$ must be gridded as 1.25 or 5/4.

(If $1\frac{1}{4}$ is gridded, it will be interpreted as $\frac{11}{4}$ not $1\frac{1}{4}$.)

- **Decimal Accuracy:** Decimal answers must be entered as accurately as possible. For example, if you obtain an answer such as 0.1666. . ., you should record the result as .166 or .167. **Less accurate values such as .16 or .17 are not acceptable.**

Acceptable ways to grid $\frac{1}{6}$ = .1666. . .

For each question, you'll see a grid with four boxes and a column of ovals, or "bubbles," beneath each. First write your numerical answer in the boxes, one digit, decimal point, or fraction sign per box. But the numbers in these boxes are there just to help you grid in properly. They're not read by the scoring computer.

172 **KAPLAN**

YOU CAN GET A POINT ONLY IF YOU CORRECTLY
FILL IN THE OVALS BELOW THE BOXES.

WARNING:

- Fill in no more than one oval per column.
- Make the oval you grid match your number above.

 MAKE SURE YOU GRID IN ONLY ONE OVAL PER
COLUMN.

FILLING IN THE GRID

The grid cannot accommodate:

- Negative answers
- Answers with variables (*x, y, w,* etc.)
- Answers greater than 9,999
- Answers with commas (write 1000, not 1,000)
- Mixed numbers (such as $2\frac{1}{2}$, which must be gridded as 5/2 or 2.5)

  RECOMMENDATION: Always start your answer in the first column box.

Technically, you can start in any column, but follow this rule to avoid mistakes. Do so even if your answer has only one or two figures. If you always start with the first column, your answers will always fit. Since there is no oval for 0 in the first column, grid an answer of 0 in any other column.

Note: If your answer is .7, don't grid 0.7! You can't grid a 0 in the first column.

 START YOUR ANSWER IN THE FIRST COLUMN BOX WHENEVER POSSIBLE.

In a Fractional Answer, Grid (/) in the Correct Column

The sign (/) separates the numerator from the denominator. It appears only in columns two and three.

> *WARNING: A fractional answer with four digits—like 31/42—won't fit.*

Change Mixed Numbers to Decimals or Fractions Before You Grid

If you try to grid a mixed number, it will be read as a fraction, and be counted wrong. For example, 4 1/2 will be read as the fraction 41/2, which is $20\frac{1}{2}$.

So first change mixed numbers to fractions or decimals, then grid in. In this case:

- Change 4 1/2 to 9/2 and grid in the fraction (as shown below)
- Or change $4\frac{1}{2}$ to 4.5 and grid in the decimal

DON'T GRID IN MIXED NUMBERS.

Watch Where You Put Your Decimal Points

- For a decimal less than 1, such as .127, enter the decimal point in the first box.
- Only put a 0 before the decimal point if it's part of the answer, as in 20.5—don't put one there (if your answer is, say, .5) just to make your answer look more accurate.
- Never grid a decimal point in the last column.

With Long or Repeating Decimals, Grid the First Three Digits Only and Plug in the Decimal Point Where It Belongs

- Say three answers are .45454545, 82.452312, and 1.428743. Grid .454, 82.4, and 1.42 respectively.

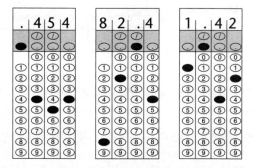

- You could round 1.428743 up to the nearest hundredth (1.43). Since it's not required, though, don't bother rounding off: You could make a mistake. Note that rounding to an even shorter answer—1.4—would be incorrect.

PART FOUR: Putting It All Together

 BE CAREFUL WITH DECIMALS. AS A RULE, DON'T
ROUND OFF. JUST CHOP OFF THE EXCESS DIGITS.

On Grid-Ins with More than One Right Answer, Choose One and Enter It

Say you're asked for a two-digit integer that is a multiple of 2, 3, and 5. You might answer 30, 60, or 90. Whichever you grid would be right.

Some Grid-Ins Have a Range of Possible Answers

Suppose you're asked to grid a value of m where $1 - 2m < m$ and $5m - 2 < m$. Solving for m in the first inequality, you find that $\frac{1}{3} < m$. Solving for m in the second inequality, you find that $m < \frac{1}{2}$. So $\frac{1}{3} < m < \frac{1}{2}$. Grid in any value between $\frac{1}{3}$ and $\frac{1}{2}$ (Gridding in $\frac{1}{3}$ or $\frac{1}{2}$ would be wrong.) When the answer is a range of values, it's often easier to work with decimals: $.333 < m < .5$. Then you can quickly grid .4 (or .35 or .45, etc.) as your answer.

 DON'T BE THROWN BY GRID-INS THAT HAVE A RANGE OF POSSIBLE ANSWERS; CHOOSE ONE AND GRID IT IN.

Write Your Answers in the Number Boxes

This doesn't get you points by itself, but you will make fewer mistakes if you write your answers in the number boxes. You may think that gridding directly will save time, but writing first, then gridding, helps ensure accuracy, which means more points.

 UNLESS YOU'RE ALMOST OUT OF TIME, DON'T TRY TO SAVE TIME BY GRIDDING WITHOUT WRITING IN THE NUMBERS FIRST. (BUT MAKE SURE YOU DO FILL IN THE OVALS.)

Grid-in Pop Quiz

(Note: This quiz tests only your gridding ability. On the actual SAT, you'll have to do a regular math problem, get the answer, and then grid it in. But here, we've already given you the answers to grid. Just fill out the grids to reflect the answers given.)

126     $\dfrac{3}{8}$ 85.9   2,143 $5\dfrac{1}{2}$

   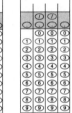

0   .141414 $\dfrac{14}{5}$ $1\dfrac{2}{3}$ 8.175

Answers

126     $\frac{3}{8}$ 85.9   2,143 $5\frac{1}{2}$

0   .141414 $\frac{14}{5}$ $1\frac{2}{3}$ 8.17

STEP ELEVEN RECAP

- You can get a point only if you correctly fill in the ovals below the boxes.
- Make sure you grid in only one oval per column.
- Start your answer in the first column box whenever possible.
- Don't grid in mixed numbers.
- Be careful with decimals. As a rule, don't round off. Just chop off the excess digits.
- Don't be thrown by Grid-ins that have a range of possible answers; choose one and grid it in.
- Unless you're almost out of time, don't try to save time by gridding without writing in the numbers first. (But make sure you do fill in the ovals).

PUTTING IT ALL TOGETHER

PUTTING IT ALL
TOGETHER

STEP 12:
END-OF-TIME TECHNIQUES

A Correct Guess Is Worth as Much as Any Other Correct Answer

Obviously, the best way to find an answer is to actually solve the problem. But if you're stuck or running out of time at the end of a section, shortcuts and guessing can be good alternatives.

All SAT questions except Grid-ins are scored to discourage random guessing. For every question you get right you earn a whole point. For every question you get wrong, you lose a fraction of a point. So if you guess at random on a number of questions, the points you gain from correct guesses are theoretically canceled out by the points you lose on incorrect guesses, for no overall gain or loss.

But you can make educated guesses. This raises the odds of guessing correctly, so the fractional points you lose no longer cancel out all the whole points you gain. You have just raised your score.

To make an educated guess, eliminate answer choices you know to be wrong, and guess from what's left. Of course, the more answer choices you can eliminate, the better chance you have of guessing the correct answer from what's left over.

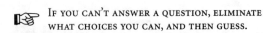 IF YOU CAN'T ANSWER A QUESTION, ELIMINATE
WHAT CHOICES YOU CAN, AND THEN GUESS.

Here are some strategies for getting quick points on the SAT Math and Verbal problems when you don't have time to really think them through.

ELIMINATE UNREASONABLE ANSWER CHOICES

Before you guess, think about the problem, and decide which answers don't make logical sense. Try this next problem.

> The ratio of men to women in a certain room is 13:11. If there are 429 men in the room, how many women are there?
>
> (A) 143
>
> (B) 363
>
> (C) 433
>
> (D) 507
>
> (E) 792

Solution:
- The ratio of men to women is 13:11, so there are more men than women.
- Since there are 429 men, there must be fewer than 429 women.
- So you can eliminate choices (C), (D), and (E).
- The answer must be either (A) or (B), so guess. The correct answer is (B).

ELIMINATE UNREASONABLE ANSWER CHOICES.

HINT: Math answer choices are typically given in increasing or decreasing order, making it easier to eliminate some choices that are way off.

ELIMINATE THE OBVIOUS ON HARD QUESTIONS

HINT: On harder questions, obvious answers are usually wrong.

On the hard questions (those that appear late in a set), obvious answers are usually wrong. So eliminate them when you guess. This rule of thumb doesn't hold true for early, easy questions, where the obvious answer is usually right.

Now apply the rule. In the following difficult problem, which obvious answer should you eliminate?

> A number *x* is increased by 30% and then the result is decreased by 20%. What is the final result of these changes?
>
> (A) *x* is increased by 10%
>
> (B) *x* is increased by 6%
>
> (C) *x* is increased by 4%
>
> (D) *x* is decreased by 5%
>
> (E) *x* is decreased by 10%

Solution:

If you picked (A) as the obvious choice to eliminate, you'd be right. Most people would combine the decrease of 20% with the increase of 30%, getting a net increase of 10%. That's the easy, obvious answer, but not the correct answer. If you must guess, avoid (A). The correct answer is (C).

 ELIMINATE EASY, OBVIOUS ANSWERS ON HARD QUESTIONS (THOSE THAT APPEAR LATE IN A SET).

This strategy also applies to Vocabulary-in-Context questions in Critical Reading. The most familiar definition of a word is rarely correct, so, in a time pinch, eliminate it.

> In line 45, *temper* most nearly means
>
> (A) disposition
>
> (B) nature
>
> (C) anger
>
> (D) mood
>
> (E) mixture

Even without reading the passage, you can guess that the right answer won't be (C), since that is the "obvious" answer.

EYEBALL LENGTHS, ANGLES, AND AREAS ON GEOMETRY PROBLEMS

Use diagrams that accompany geometry problems to help you eliminate wrong answer choices. First make sure that the diagram is drawn to scale. If it is, estimate quantities or eyeball the diagram. Then eliminate answer choices that seem way too large or too small.

Diagrams are always drawn to scale unless there's a note like this: "Note: Figure not drawn to scale." If you see this note, *don't* use this strategy.

LENGTHS

When a geometry question asks for a length, use the given lengths to estimate the unknown length. Measure off the given length by making a nick in your pencil with your thumbnail (you're not allowed to bring a ruler). Then hold the pencil against the unknown length on the diagram to see how the lengths compare.

In the following problem, which answer choices can you eliminate by eyeballing?

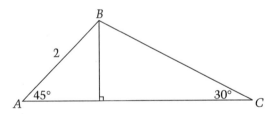

In the figure above, what is the length of *BC* ?

(A) $\sqrt{2}$

(B) 2

(C) $2\sqrt{2}$

(D) 4

(E) $4\sqrt{2}$

PART FOUR: Putting It All Together

Solution:

- *AB* is 2, so measure off this length on your pencil.
- Compare *BC* with this length.
- *BC* appears almost twice as long as *AB*, so *BC* is about 4.
- Since 2 is about 1.4, choices (A) and (B) are too small.
- Choice (E) is much greater than 4, so eliminate that.
- Now guess between (C) and (D). The correct answer is (C).

ANGLES

You can also eyeball angles. To eyeball an angle, compare the angle with a familiar angle, such as a straight angle (180°), a right angle (90°), or half a right angle (45°). The corner of your answer grid is a right angle, so use that to see if an angle is greater or less than 90° (but be careful not to make any stray marks on your answer grid!).

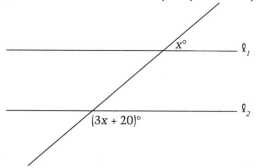

In the figure above, if line 1 ∥ line 2, what is the value of *x*?

(A) 130

(B) 100

(C)   80

(D)   50

(E)   40

Solution:
- You see that x is less than 90 degrees, so eliminate choices (A) and (B).
- Since x appears to be much less than 90 degrees, eliminate choice (C).
- Now pick between (D) and (E). In fact, the correct answer is (E).

AREAS

Eyeballing an area is similar to eyeballing a length. You compare an unknown area in a diagram to an area that you do know.

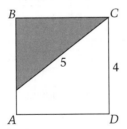

In square *ABCD* above, what is the area of the shaded region?

(A)   10

(B)   9

(C)   8

  (D) 6

  (E) 4

Solution:

- Since *ABCD* is a square, it has area 4^2, or 16.
- The shaded area is less than half the size of the square, so its area must be less than 8.
- Eliminate answer choices (A), (B), and (C). The correct answer
  is (D).

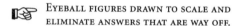 EYEBALL FIGURES DRAWN TO SCALE AND ELIMINATE ANSWERS THAT ARE WAY OFF.

FIND THE RANGE AND GUESS ON GRID-INS

On Grid-ins, there are no answer choices to eliminate, but Grid-ins are the only questions on which you won't lose points for guessing wrong. So, if you're stuck, try to estimate the general range of the answer, and guess.

See if you can guess intelligently on the following hard Grid-in.

> A triangle has one side of length 3 and another of length 7.
> If the length of the longest side is a solution to the equation
> $x^2 - 2x = 63$, what is the length of the longest side?

Solution:

Even if you can't solve that quadratic, you know that the sum of any two sides of a triangle must be greater than the length of the third side. So the third side must be less than 7 + 3, or 10, but greater than 7 (since it is the longest side). Since solutions to SAT quadratics are usually integers, pick an integer between 7 and 10. If you picked 9, you'd be right.

 NEVER LEAVE A GRID-IN BLANK. FIND AN APPROXIMATE RANGE FOR THE ANSWER AND GUESS. THERE'S NO PENALTY!

LOOK FOR THE FAST POINTS IN CRITICAL READING

What do you do if you find yourself a minute from the end of a verbal section with one Critical Reading passage still totally unread? Skip the passage entirely and go for the quick points. Here's what you should look for.

Vocabulary-in-Context Questions

These questions always have a line reference. Read the cited part of the passage and then decide which choice would be the best substitute for the keyed word.

Little Picture Questions

Find the ones with specific line references. Read around the cited part of the passage and then answer the question as well as you can.

 IF YOU DON'T HAVE TIME TO READ A CRITICAL READING PASSAGE, SKIP THE PASSAGE AND TRY TO ANSWER THE VOCABULARY-IN-CONTEXT QUESTIONS FIRST, THEN THE LITTLE PICTURE QUESTIONS.

STEP TWELVE RECAP

- If you can't answer a question, eliminate as many choices as you can, and then guess.
- Eliminate unreasonable answer choices.
- Eliminate easy, obvious answers on hard questions (those that appear late in a set).
- Eyeball figures drawn to scale and eliminate answers that are way off.
- Never leave a Grid-in blank. Find an approximate range for the answer and guess. There is no penalty for an incorrect response.
- If you don't have time to read a Critical Reading passage, skip the passage and try to answer the Vocabulary-in-Context questions first, then the Little Picture questions.

STEP 13:
LAST-MINUTE TIPS

AND NOW . . . THE SAT

Is it starting to feel like your whole life is a buildup to the SAT? You've known about it for years, worried about it for months, and now you've spent at least a few hours in solid preparation for it. As the test gets closer, you may find your anxiety is on the rise. You shouldn't worry. After the preparation you've received from this book, you're in good shape for Test Day.

To calm any pre-test jitters you may have, let's go over a few strategies for the couple of days before and after the test.

THREE DAYS BEFORE THE TEST

If you've left yourself this much time, take a full-length practice test under timed conditions. This can be an actual published SAT or one of the practice tests contained in Kaplan's books on the test. If it's a full week before the test, you may even be able to go to the local Kaplan educational center to take a free diagnostic practice SAT. Call 1-800-KAP-TEST to find the Kaplan center nearest you.

Try to use all of the techniques and tips you've learned in this book. Approach the test strategically, actively, and confidently.

> *WARNING: Don't take a full practice SAT if you have less than 48 hours left before the test. Doing so will probably exhaust you, hurting your scoring potential on the actual test! You wouldn't run a marathon the day before the real thing, would you?*

TWO DAYS BEFORE THE TEST

Go over the results of your practice test. Don't worry too much about your score or whether you got a specific question right or wrong. The practice test doesn't count, remember. But do examine your performance on specific questions with an eye to how you might get through each one faster and with greater accuracy on the actual test to come.

After reviewing your test, look over the Recap at the end of each step.

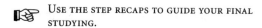 USE THE STEP RECAPS TO GUIDE YOUR FINAL STUDYING.

THE NIGHT BEFORE THE TEST: DON'T STUDY

Get together an "SAT survival kit" containing the following items:

- Calculator with fresh batteries
- Watch
- Few No. 2 pencils (pencils with slightly dull points fill the ovals better)
- Erasers
- Photo ID card
- Your admission ticket from ETS
- Snack—there are two breaks, and you'll probably get hungry

 ASSEMBLE AN "SAT SURVIVAL KIT."

Know exactly where you're going, exactly how you're getting there, and exactly how long it takes to get there. It's probably a good idea to visit your test center sometime before Test Day, so that you know what to expect—what the rooms are like, how the desks are set up, and so on.

Relax the night before the test. Read a good book, take a bubble bath, watch TV. Get a good night's sleep. Go to bed early and leave yourself extra time in the morning.

 DON'T STUDY THE NIGHT BEFORE THE TEST.

THE MORNING OF THE TEST

- Eat breakfast. Make it something substantial, but not anything too heavy or greasy.
- Don't drink a lot of coffee if you're not used to it; bathroom breaks cut into your time, and too much caffeine is a bad idea.
- Dress in layers so that you can adjust to the temperature of the test room.

 DRESS IN LAYERS.

- Read something. Warm up your brain with a newspaper or a magazine. You shouldn't let the SAT be the first thing you read that day.

 WARM UP YOUR BRAIN BY READING SOMETHING.

- Be sure to get there early. Allow yourself extra time for traffic, mass transit delays, and/or detours around people (like your old algebra teacher) who might only add to your stress level if you stopped to talk to them.

DURING THE TEST

Don't be shaken. If you find your confidence slipping, remind yourself how well you've prepared. You know the structure of the test; you know the instructions; you've had practice with—and have learned strategies for—every question type.

Even if something goes really wrong, don't panic. If the test booklet is defective—two pages are stuck together or the ink has run—try to stay calm. Raise your hand and tell the proctor you need a new book. If you accidentally misgrid your answer page or put the answers in the wrong section, again *don't panic*. Raise your hand and tell the proctor. He or she might be able to arrange for you to re-grid your test after it's over, when it won't cost you any time.

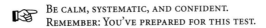 BE CALM, SYSTEMATIC, AND CONFIDENT.
REMEMBER: YOU'VE PREPARED FOR THIS TEST.

Don't think about which section is experimental. Remember, you never know for sure which section won't count. Besides, you can't work on any other section during that section's designated time slot.

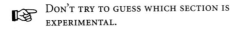 DON'T TRY TO GUESS WHICH SECTION IS
EXPERIMENTAL.

AFTER THE TEST

Once the test is over, put it out of your mind. If you don't plan to take the test again, shelve this book and start thinking about more interesting things.

You might walk out of the SAT thinking that you blew it. This is a normal reaction. Lots of people—even the highest scorers—feel that way. You tend to remember the questions that stumped you, not the many that you knew.

You can also call ETS within 24 hours to find out about canceling your score. But there is usually no good reason to do so. Remember, colleges typically accept your highest SAT score. And no test experience is going to be perfect. If you were distracted by the proctor's hacking cough this time around, next time you may be even more distracted by construction noise, or a cold, or the hideous lime-green sweater of the person sitting in front of you.

 DON'T CANCEL YOUR SCORE UNLESS YOU HAVE A
GOOD REASON TO. BUT IF YOU DO HAVE A GOOD
REASON, DO IT..

POST-SAT FESTIVITIES

After all the hard work you've put in preparing for and taking the SAT, you want to make sure you take time to celebrate afterward. Plan to get together with friends the evening after the test. Relax, have fun, let loose. After all, you've got lots to celebrate: You prepared for the test ahead of time. You did your best. You're going to get a good score.

So start thinking about all of the great parties you'll be attending at the college of your choice!

 PLAN YOUR SAT VICTORY PARTY.

STEP THIRTEEN RECAP

- Use the Step Recaps to guide your final studying.
- Assemble an "SAT Survival Kit."
- Don't study the night before the test.
- Dress in layers.
- Warm up your brain by reading something.
- Be calm, systematic, and confident. Remember: You've prepared for this test.
- Don't try to guess which section of the test is experimental.
- Don't cancel your score unless you have a good reason, but if you do need to cancel, call us.
- Plan your SAT victory party.

PART FIVE

TAKING THE PSAT

WHAT IS THE **PSAT?**

You've learned a lot about the SAT as you've worked through this book. But what if you're taking the PSAT? Here's the good news: if you're taking the PSAT, you're already in great shape, because virtually all of the techniques and strategies that apply to the SAT *also* apply to the PSAT. The one major difference between the SAT and PSAT is that the PSAT has a Writing Skills section. We'll focus on the Writing Skills section in this chapter, reviewing the grammar rules, skills, and strategies you need for success on this new section.

The PSAT (formally known as the PSAT/NMSQT or Preliminary Scholastic Assessment Test/National Merit Scholarship Qualifying Test) has two main functions. First, the PSAT serves as valuable practice for the SAT. Although shorter in duration than the actual SAT, the PSAT contains the same variety of math and verbal question types as the SAT and seeks to measure the same skills. And because your PSAT scores are not sent to colleges, you can use the PSAT to practice the skills you'll need for the SAT.

THE NATIONAL MERIT PROGRAM

The PSAT/NMSQT also provides students with a chance to qualify for National Merit Scholarship Corporation programs. If you're one of the highest scorers in your state (typically this means scoring above the 99th percentile), you may be one of 50,000 juniors chosen to enter the competition for National Merit scholarships and recognition letters. Qualifying for the program can be the first stepping stone to academic success, increasing your chances of acceptance at top-tier universities and helping you meet the financial demands of college life. Through the National Merit program, approximately 25,000 students every year receive letters of commendation and nearly 8,500 students receive scholarships.

STRUCTURE OF THE TEST

There are five sections on the PSAT: two 25-minute-long Math sections, two 25-minute-long Verbal sections, and one 30-minute-long Writing section.

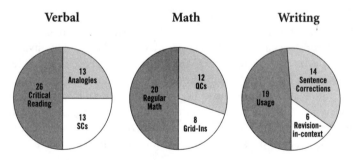

Students will receive scaled scores for Math, Verbal, and Writing in the 20–80 range. To calculate your National Merit qualifying score, simply add your Math, Verbal, and Writing scaled scores (M + V + W). The maximum score on the PSAT is 240.

THE WRITING
SKILLS SECTION

The PSAT has a special section devoted to Writing Skills. Here is what you'll need to know to get a good score.

FORMAT AND INSTRUCTIONS

The key phrase to focus on here is *multiple-choice*. In spite of its name, this new Writing Skills section doesn't actually *test* your writing ability. You're not required to produce a writing sample. Instead, you're asked to demonstrate your knowledge of the elements of good writing: correct grammar, accurate sentence structure, and paragraph construction.

Here's a great way to make the Writing Skills section easier: get familiar with the directions. Since the instructions are always the same from test to test, there is no reason to waste time reading them on the day of the test. By learning them ahead of time, you will save yourself some time on test day, and time is everything. Every second that you save while taking the test is a second that you can use to recheck your work, and tackle the questions that you saved for last. So spend some time going over the test instructions that we provide and explain here.

USAGE QUESTIONS

You'll encounter 19 Usage questions on the Writing Skills section. The directions for Usage questions look like this:

DIRECTIONS: Choose the <u>one underlined part</u> that must be changed to make the sentence correct and fill in the corresponding oval on your answer grid. If there is no error, fill in oval E.

1. For <u>a number of</u> years, Gauguin was a friend
       A

  <u>of the painter</u> Van Gogh; <u>they</u> met at <u>his</u> exhibition in
      B   C   D

Paris. <u>No error</u>
      E

Ⓐ Ⓑ Ⓒ Ⓓ Ⓔ

Usage questions require you to "spot the mistake." You're given a sentence like the one above in which certain words or phrases are underlined. Your job is to look at the underlined portions of the sentence, and to figure out which part is grammatically incorrect. For those sentences that contain no errors, and there will be some, choose choice (E), or "No error," as your answer.

Usage questions test your ability to catch words or phrases that are frequently used incorrectly in students' essays. If you are able to spot errors in word and phrase usage, the test makers assume that you are capable of using appropriate words and phrases in your own writing. In the example above, the correct answer is (D), since the ambiguous pronoun *his* doesn't indicate at whose exhibition the two painters met.

SENTENCE CORRECTION QUESTIONS

There are 14 Sentence Correction questions on the PSAT. The directions for them look like this:

DIRECTIONS: Select the choice that best expresses the meaning of the original sentence. If the original sentence is better than any of the alternative phrasings, choose A; otherwise, select one of the alternatives.

To the surprise of the school's staff, the new freshman class at Ravenswood High <u>being larger than last year's</u>.

(A) being larger than last year's

(B) is large more so than last year

(C) which is larger than the one last year

(D) is larger than last year's

(E) by far larger than the last

In Sentence Correction questions, your job is to figure out whether the underlined portion of the sentence is grammatically correct. If the sentence is correct, pick answer choice (A), which will always be identical to the original sentence. If the sentence is grammatically flawed, you will need to pick the answer choice that best *corrects* the error.

Sentence Correction questions test your ability to identify and correct sentence-structure problems that often appear in students' essays. Again, the test makers assume that if you are able to spot poorly constructed sentences and fix them, then you can probably write good sentences on your own. In the question above, the correct answer is choice (D). The verb *being* is in the wrong form, creating a run-on sentence. Choice (D) solves the problem in straight-forward fashion.

REVISION-IN-CONTEXT QUESTIONS

Here are the directions for the Revision-in-Context questions. There is only one Revision-in-Context passage on the test, accompanied by six questions.

DIRECTIONS: Read the essay and answer the questions that follow it. Pick the answer that most effectively conveys the author's meaning and follows the rules of standard written English.

(1) The school board recently took a controversial vote to allow advertising at Midville High. (2) Many disagree with this decision. (3) I do not. (4) As a member of the student council, it is important to make up for the shortfall in our school budget. (5) And we cannot afford the luxury of worrying about where the money is coming from.

Which of the following is the best way to revise and combine sentences 2 and 3 (reproduced below).

Many disagree with this decision. I do not.

(A) Many disagreeing with this decision, I am not.

(B) In contrast to the case that many that are disagreeing with this decision, I do not.

(C) Although many disagree with this decision, I do not.

(D) Even though many disagree with this decision, I am agreeing.

(E) Many disagree with this decision, but not me.

Ⓐ Ⓑ Ⓒ Ⓓ Ⓔ

You'll have noticed that Usage questions focus on words or phrases, and Sentence Corrections focus on whole sentences. In contrast, Revision-in-Context questions ask you to focus on whole *paragraphs*. In this section of the test, you will be given a passage whose individual sentences are numbered. You are then asked a series of questions about the passage. Some of the questions ask you to correct the structure or style of a particular sentence, to make it better fit into the passage as a whole. Other questions will ask you to make the passage clearer or more logical in development.

Usage and Sentence Correction questions test your ability to write accurate sentences. But good writing involves more than that. To write well, you need to be able to develop an idea or a thought into a well-constructed paragraph. Revision-in-Context questions test your ability to spot and correct logical flaws in a passage that contains errors commonly found in students' essays. If you can fix this sample passage, the test makers assume you can probably do the same thing to your own writing.

In the question above, the correct answer is (C). Sentences 2 and 3 sound choppy in their original form. Choice (C) neatly combines them together while remaining grammatically accurate and retaining the author's meaning.

THE KAPLAN THREE-STEP METHOD

Now that you are clear on the format and directions, you'll want to spend some time learning more about how to answer each question type. As with the Math and Verbal sections, the first thing you should realize about Writing questions is that you don't want to dive head first into the answer choices. Instead, you want to be systematic, and use a consistent, strategic method for each question. Without this book, you could spend hours trying to figure out the right methods to use. Chances are, you don't have that kind of time. Don't worry. Here's what you need to do:

1. **Read the sentence, "listening" for a mistake.**
2. **Identify the error.**
3. **Check the answer choices.**

USAGE QUESTIONS

How do you listen for an error? If English is your native language, you already have an innate sense of grammar. No doubt you've often heard someone say something that didn't sound right; you could tell that the speaker used the wrong word, or used it in the wrong way. That's the approach you should take to Usage questions. By listening to the sentence in your mind as you read, you will be able to hear the error, if there is one.

Read the following question, applying the Kaplan Three-Step Method.

Early <u>experience</u> of racial discrimination <u>made</u> an
       A   B

<u>indelible</u> <u>impression for</u> the late Supreme Court
  C   D

Justice Thurgood Marshall. <u>No error</u>
                          E

When you read the question, did you hear a mistake? If so, you are done with the question. On the test, you would just fill in the corresponding oval and move on. If you didn't hear the mistake, just go back and read each underlined part again. The word *experience* sounds fine. The word *made* seems fine in terms of subject verb agreement. And the word *indelible* also sounds fine. However, the phrase *impression for* sounds wrong. The correct phrase to use would be *impression on*, making choice (D) the correct answer.

This question was a classic example of an incorrect preposition. Let's take a look at some of the classic errors that appear on the Usage section.

Verb Tense Errors

In English grammar, verb tense indicates when an action is taking place—past, present, or future. You don't need to know the names of different tenses for the PSAT, but you do need to know how to use them. Take a look at the following sentence.

> Because I was in the shower, I was missing your call.

Sounds awkward, doesn't it? That's because *was missing* is in the wrong tense. Take a look at the following sentence.

> Because I was in the shower, I <u>missed</u> your call.

That sounds much better doesn't it? By changing *was missing* to *missed* the sentence was easily fixed. A number of Usage questions on the PSAT will require you to spot mistakes in verb tense.

Subject-Verb Agreement Errors

Another common mistake on the PSAT has to do with subject-verb agreement. In standard written English, the subject and verb in each sentence must "agree" in person and in number. In other words, if the subject is singular, it must take the singular form of the verb;

likewise for the plural forms. Also, the correct verb form is based on whether the subject is in the first-, second-, or third-person form. Take a look at the following sentence:

> Coming from a rural community, Orville were not
> accustomed to the pace of the big city.

The name Orville aside, this sentence sounds pretty strange, doesn't it? That's because the verb *were* does not agree with the subject *Orville.* Now look at the following:

> Coming from a rural community, Orville <u>was</u> not accustomed
> to the pace of the big city.

The sentence sounds much better after *were* is replaced with *was.*

Pronoun Errors

Another very common error that is tested on the PSAT is the misuse of pronouns. In English grammar, pronouns must agree with their antecedents (the nouns that precede them) in both case and number. Try reading the following sentence:

> A person who spends all their money may be in danger of
> financial ruin.

This sentence is a good example of a very common error. In an effort to be "gender neutral" a lot of people use the pronoun *they* or *their* to refer to a person of unknown gender. Unfortunately, this creates grammatical problems, since *their* is plural, and *a person* is singular. The sentence should read as follows.

> A person who spends all <u>his</u> money may be in danger of
> financial ruin.

OR

A person who spends all <u>her</u> money may be in danger of financial ruin.

Case and Number Errors

The case of a pronoun is the form in which it appears—for example, *he* as opposed to *him.* The number of a pronoun is exactly what it sounds like— singular or plural. *She* is a singular pronoun; *they* is plural.

Give this question a try.

There <u>was</u> a huge public outcry <u>over</u> the cruel methods
     A   B

<u>employed</u> at the animal pound, but in the end, nothing came
  C

of <u>them</u>. <u>No error</u>.
   D   E

Since *outcry* is singular and *them* is plural, you have a situation in which the pronoun does not agree with its antecedent. If you replace *them* with *it,* the sentence becomes correct.

Preposition and Connective Errors

The Usage section often tests your ability to choose the right preposition. Prepositions are the little words that connect sentences together. Often, if you choose the wrong preposition in a sentence, then the meaning of the sentence becomes vague or illogical. Take a look at the following sentence:

I don't like to argue between my friends.

This sounds a little strange doesn't it? That's because *with* is the preposition most commonly used with the verb *to argue* in English.

To argue with someone is to be engaged in an argument with that person. Read the following:

> I don't like to argue <u>with</u> my friends.

This sounds much better, doesn't it? As you can see, just a small word can drastically change a sentence. The PSAT will include questions that test your ability to spot the incorrect use of these small words.

Comparison Errors

Here's something that you may not have known about standard written English. When you compare two or more parts of speech (for example, nouns or verb phrases) you should make sure you're comparing the same parts of speech in the same form. Take this example:

> The technician agreed that fixing a television is easier than computer repair.

Even though you can understand what this sentence is trying to communicate, it should sound a bit labored and clumsy. That's because the two elements that are being compared, *fixing a television* and *computer repair,* are not in the same form. The first half of the sentence includes a verb, and the second half does not. The sentence would be better if it were written as follows.

> The technician agreed that fixing a television is easier than <u>repairing computers</u>.

In this case, *fixing a television* and *repairing computers* are both in the same form—that is, they both have verbs that are in the same form.

Adjective and Adverb Errors

Adjectives are words that modify or describe nouns and pronouns. Adverbs are words that modify verbs, adjectives, or other adverbs. In the phrase *the ugly dog*, the word *ugly* is an adjective. In the phrase *he drove fast*, the word *fast* is an adverb. On the PSAT, the test makers like to find out whether you can identify commonly confused adjectives and adverbs. Take a look at the following sentence:

> Sam studied hard for the test, so he did good.

This sentence is a good example of a commonly misused adjective. In this sentence, *good* is used to modify the verb *did*. But the word *good* is an adjective, not an adverb. The sentence should read as follows.

> Sam studied hard for the test, so he did well.

In this sentence, the error has been corrected. The word *well* is an adverb, and can be used to modify the verb *did*.

Double Negatives

If a sentence contains two negatives (words such as *not* or *without*) they create a double negative and cancel each other out. It's sort of like math, in which two negatives make a positive. Read the following sentence.

> Peggy can't have none of that food because she's allergic to it.

In this sentence, there are two negatives—*can't* and *none*. Because these two negatives are in the same sentence, they cancel each other out. In other words, the sentence is saying that Peggy cannot have none of that food, meaning that she must have that food. This conveys a meaning that is the opposite of the meaning that the sentence was trying to convey. Even though you can understand the meaning of the sentence, this redundancy contradicts the rules of standard written English and therefore is incorrect. The sentence should read as follows.

Peggy can't have <u>any</u> of that food because she's allergic to it.

SENTENCE CORRECTION QUESTIONS

As was the case with Usage questions, you should also approach Sentence Correction questions as strategically as possible. The most effective way to do this is to follow the Kaplan Three-Step Method for Sentence Corrections.

  1. Read the sentence, listening for a mistake.
  2. Predict a correction.
  3. Select the answer choice that matches your prediction, while eliminating clearly wrong answer choices.

Try reading through the following question, applying the Kaplan Three-Step Method.

In the Middle Ages, when astronomical phenomena were poorly understood, <u>the comets that seemed to portend</u> military conflicts or other social crises.

(A) the comets that seemed to portend

(B) the comets that seeming to portend

(C) the comets seemed to portend

(D) the comets apparently portending

(E) and when the comets seemed to portend

When you read through the question, did you hear a mistake? You probably noticed that *the comets that seemed to portend* sounded strange; the sentence ended without really completing a thought. Now that you have found the error, you should try to fix it. How could you make the sentence sound more complete? The word *that* is unnecessary, isn't it? Now that you have corrected the question, find the answer choice which best matches your prediction. You can eliminate choice (A) because that just restates what is already in the passage. The correct choice is choice (C), which matches your prediction.

CLASSIC SENTENCE CORRECTION ERRORS

The next few pages list the most common types of errors found in Sentence Sentence Correction questions. You should work through this section, making sure that you understand what is wrong with each question.

Sentence Fragments

A sentence fragment is exactly what it sounds like—a fragment of a sentence. To put it another way, a sentence fragment is an incomplete sentence. It may look like a sentence, but it is either grammatically incomplete because it lacks a main subject or a verb, or logically incomplete because it lacks the necessary elements to express a complete thought. Take a look at the following sentence:

Eggs and fresh vegetables on sale at the farmer's market.

It doesn't sound complete, does it? It sounds strange because it's missing a verb. If you read the following out loud, it will sound much better.

> Eggs and fresh vegetables <u>are</u> on sale at the
> farmer's market.

By including the verb *are* the sentence becomes complete.

Run-on Sentences

Run-on sentences occur when two complete sentences that should
be separate are joined together. Here are two examples:

> Winston Churchill is one of the twentieth century's most
> admired politicians, his speeches are still quoted today.

> Winston Churchill is one of the twentieth century's most
> admired politicians his speeches are still quoted today.

You can tell that the above two examples are run-on sentences
because they sound like they *should be* two sentences. Once again,
your ear will be crucial to helping you in this section.

There are three ways that you can fix a run-on sentence.

1. Use a period:

> Winston Churchill is one of the twentieth century's most
> admired politicians. His speeches are still quoted today.

2. Use a conjunction/make one sentence dependent:

> Because Winston Churchill is one of the twentieth century's
> most admired politicians, his speeches are still quoted
> today.

3. Use a semicolon:

> Winston Churchill is one of the twentieth century's most
> admired politicians; his speeches are still quoted today.

You need to be aware of these three ways to fix run-on sentences as you work through Sentence Corrections.

Coordination/Subordination Errors

Coordination and subordination errors are those in which clauses are joined together incorrectly. Faulty coordination and subordination are closely related to each other, but they require separate explanations.

Faulty Coordination. Faulty coordination occurs when the word (or words) joining two sentences together does not express the right logical relationship. Here's an example:

Wrong: Because he was very unhappy, he smiled all the time.

Correct: <u>Although</u> he was very unhappy, he smiled all the time.

In these examples, it made no sense to say that "because he was unhappy, he smiled." But the second sentence corrects this problem by switching the word *because* with the word *although.*

Faulty Subordination. Faulty subordination is an error that is similar to a sentence fragment. When a group of words contains two or more dependent clauses, but no independent clause, you have faulty subordination. To look at it another way, faulty subordination occurs when a group of words is not anchored to a complete thought. Take a look at the following sentence.

Walking into the kitchen in my sleep and opening the refrigerator.

This sounds awkward, doesn't it? Now read the following.

> I walked into the kitchen in my sleep and opened
> the refrigerator.

See the difference? In the first example, the verbs *walking* and *opening* made the sentence incomplete. By changing *walking* to *I walked* and *opening* to *opened* in the second example, the sentence becomes a complete sentence.

Modifier Errors

Modifiers are phrases that provide extra information about nouns and verbs in a sentence. The tricky thing about a modifier is that it must appear next to the word or words that it is modifying. Take a look at the following example.

> Designed for small children, Ed had to stoop to reach the
> water fountain.

The sentence sounds funny, doesn't it? You know what the sentence is trying to say. But the way in which it is written makes it sound like Ed was designed for small children (a scary thought, whoever Ed is). Notice how differently the sentence sounds now:

> Ed had to stoop to reach the water fountain, which was
> designed for small children.

By moving the modifier *designed for small children* to the end of the sentence, we were able to make the meaning of this sentence totally clear.

Parallelism Errors

Parallelism is a lot like the comparisons that appeared earlier in this chapter. Parallelism refers to the rule that when you list items, they should be in the same form. Take a look at the following sentence.

> To conserve calories, to promote digestion, or so that they are less vulnerable to predators, wild animals rest during many of their waking hours.

Although you can understand the meaning of this sentence, it sounds a little awkward. This is because the items listed, "to conserve calories, to promote digestion or so that they are less vulnerable," are not parallel. Two of the items start with the word *to* while the third item does not. The sentence should read:

> <u>To conserve</u> calories, <u>to promote</u> digestion, or <u>to be less vulnerable to</u> predators, wild animals rest during many of their waking hours.

Can you hear the difference between the two sentences?

REVISION-IN-CONTEXT QUESTIONS

Don't let the fact that you have to read a whole paragraph to answer Revision-in-Context questions scare you. This portion of the test is actually not that hard. If you can do Usage questions and Sentence Correction questions, you will be in fine shape to tackle Revision-in-Context questions.

There are two things to keep in mind as you tackle Revision-in-Context questions. The first thing is that you should understand the point of these questions. The test makers want you to be able to write a concise, stylistically smooth, and logical essay. Every question that they ask you will be geared towards this purpose. The second thing you should keep in mind as you work is Kaplan's Three-Step Method:

1. Read the essay. As in Critical Reading, you need to get a sense of the essay's overall main idea and the main idea of each paragraph.

2. Read the question stem. Understand what the question wants you to do. Questions that require you to revise or combine sentences will supply the sentence numbers to you. Questions that ask about the entire essay generally won't refer to specific sentences.

3. Reread the relevant portion of the essay. Reread the sentences before and after the affected sentence(s). Rereading the lines around the affected sentence(s) will provide you with a sense of context, which will help you to choose the best construction from the answer choices.

Let's try applying the Kaplan Three-Step Method. As Step One, take a look at the passage below, and try to figure out what the author's main idea is.

(1) While watching skateboarders in a shopping mall, people sometimes shake their heads. (2) They shake their heads since because they think that skateboarders are bad kids and that the sport should be banned. (3) I think that skateboarding is a great sport. (4) It allows young people to be physically active, without doing something harmful to him. (5) Kids have a lot of energy that needs to be burned off. (6) All you have to do is to read the paper. (7) And if you did that, you would see that kids are getting into serious trouble everywhere, sometimes even killing people. (8) But skateboarders have found a way to burn off their energy in a way that is fun and in something that is challenging because it is physically hard. (9) A lot of adults worry that skateboarders are bad because they tend to mark up civic property, scuff buildings and even tear chunks out of staircases. (10) This is true sometimes. (11) Similarly I believe that that the best solution to this problem would be if the city acknowledged the positive aspects of skateboarding, and built more skateboard parks. (12) Then

kids would have a place to go and skate, and adults wouldn't
have to worry about parks and private property.

Did you figure out what the point of the passage was as you read? The author is trying to explain why skateboarding is worthwhile and healthy, in spite of the negative view that some people have of the sport.

You may even have noticed a few errors while you were reading. But don't bother trying to correct anything yet. You can make a small mark to note errors if you want to, but don't spend too much time on those errors. The purpose of your first read-through should be just to get you acquainted with the passage.

There are three types of Revision-in-Context questions.

- Sentence revision
- Sentence combination
- Logic and clarity

Now that you have read the passage, let's take a look at the first of these three question types.

Sentence Revision

Step Two of the Kaplan Three-Step Method is to read the question stem. Here is a typical sentence-revision question.

Which of the following is the best way to revise the underlined portion of sentence 3?

I think that skateboarding is a great sport.

(A) Believing that, I

(B) Because of this, I

(C) However, I

(D) Unfortunately, I

(E) Furthermore, I

This question asks you to revise a sentence in the passage. Notice that the sentence is reprinted below the question itself. After you have read the question stem, and understand what it wants you to do, you should apply Step Three of the Three-Step Method—reread the relevant portion of the essay. You should read just enough of the passage to figure out the context in which this sentence fits. The author starts out the passage by explaining that some people do not like skateboarding. He then goes on to say that he likes the sport. However, the author did not make a smooth transition between these two opposing ideas. He needed to do something to make the paragraph flow better. Can you see which answer choice would make this transition? If you picked choice (C), you are right. Starting sentence 3 with the word *however* would make the paragraph stylistically much better.

The test makers believe that one of the most important aspects of writing involves clear and accurate sentence structure. Keep in mind the grammatical errors that we discussed in the sections on Usage and Sentence Correction questions, and you should do fine on this question type.

Sentence Combination

Now take a look at this question.

Which of the following is the best way to combine sentences 1 and 2 (reproduced below)?

While watching skateboarders in a shopping mall, people sometimes shake their heads. They shake their heads since because they think that skateboarders are bad kids and that the sport should be banned.

(A) While watching skateboarders in a shopping mall, people sometimes shake their heads: they shake their heads because they think that skateboarders are bad kids and that the sport should be banned.

(B) While watching skateboarders in a shopping mall, people sometimes shake their heads, because they think that skateboarders are bad kids and that the sport should be banned.

(C) While watching skateboarders in a shopping mall, people sometimes shake their heads because they skateboarders are bad kids and the sport should be banned.

(D) While watching skateboarders in a shopping mall, people sometimes shake their heads and they think that skateboarders are bad kids and that the sport should be banned.

(E) While watching skateboarders in a shopping mall, people sometimes shake their heads thinking that skateboarders are bad kids and that the sport should be banned.

This question asks you to combine two sentences together. Can you see why? These two sentences sound choppy and uneven. Also, the author repeats the phrase *shake their heads*. Can you see which answer choice fixes this problem? If you chose choice (B), you were right. Choice (B) combines the sentences together, by including the word *because*.

Remember that the test makers believe that a well-written essay avoids wordiness and redundancy. Also remember that correct answers will always be grammatically and logically correct.

Logic and Clarity

Another kind of question tests your ability to spot gaps in the author's logic and clarity. Take a look at the following question.

> The writer of the passage could best improve sentence 10 by
>
> (A) acknowledging the weakness of his argument
>
> (B) providing a specific example
>
> (C) highlighting his opinion
>
> (D) discussing an example that is counter to his thesis
>
> (E) mentioning the other youth activities

The question asks you how sentence 10 could be improved. To figure out the answer to this question, you need to remember to do Step Three of the Kaplan Three-Step Method. Go back and read the portion of the passage that this sentence appeared in.

Can you see the flaw in the sentence after rereading it? The author starts to say in sentence 9 that some people believe that skateboarders are destructive to private property. In sentence 10, the author says that this is true sometimes. In sentence 11, the author starts to discuss "the city." The problem is that the author moves to abruptly from one point to another. Furthermore, since this is an essay expressing an opinion, he needs to back up his opinion when he can. The problem with sentence 10 is that the author does not fully explain what he means, making choice (B) the correct answer.

GETTING READY FOR THE **PSAT**

If you were easily able to work through this material, then you should do fine on the PSAT's new Writing Skills section. But if you feel that you need a little more grammar practice, you might want to check out Kaplan's *SAT II: Writing* book, which contains a wealth of grammar material with detailed explanations and drills. But whether or not you chose to supplement your preparation, you should realize that by preparing as much as you have, you're in much better shape for the day of the test!

APPENDIX

THE KAPLAN ADVANTAGE™ STRESS MANAGEMENT SYSTEM

The countdown has begun. Your date with THE TEST is looming on the horizon. Anxiety is on the rise. Butterflies in your stomach have gone ballistic. Perhaps you feel as if the last thing you ate has turned into a lead ball. Your thinking is getting cloudy. Maybe you think you won't be ready. Maybe you already know your stuff, but you're going into panic mode anyway. Worst of all, you're not sure of what to do about it.

Don't freak! It is possible to tame that anxiety and stress—before and during the SAT or any other test. We'll show you how. You won't believe how quickly and easily you can deal with that killer anxiety.

MAKING THE MOST OF YOUR PREP TIME

Lack of control is one of the prime causes of stress. A ton of research shows that if you don't have a sense of control over what's happening in your life you can easily end up feeling helpless and hopeless. So, just having concrete things to do and to think about—taking control—will help reduce your stress. This section shows you how to take control during the days leading up to the test.

IDENTIFY THE SOURCES OF STRESS

In the space provided, jot down (in pencil) anything you identify as a source of your test-related stress. The idea is to pin down that free-floating anxiety so that you can take control of it. Here are some common examples to get you started.

- I always freeze up on tests.
- I'm nervous about the math (or the grammar or reading comp, etc.).
- I need a good/great score to go to Such-and-Such University.
- My older brother/sister/best friend/girl- or boyfriend did really well. I *must* match their scores or do better.
- My parents/boss, who are paying for the course/school, will be really disappointed if I don't test well.
- I'm afraid of losing my focus and concentration.
- I'm afraid I'm not spending enough time preparing.
- I study like crazy but nothing seems to stick in my mind.
- I always run out of time and get panicky.
- I feel as though thinking is becoming like wading through thick mud.

Sources of Stress

_____

_____

_____

_____

_____

_____

_____

_____

_____

_____

Take a few minutes to think about the things you've just written down. Then put them in some sort of order. List the statements you most associate with your stress and anxiety first, and put the least disturbing items last. Chances are, the top of the list is a fairly accurate description of exactly how you react to test anxiety, both physically and mentally. The later items usually describe your fears (disappointing mom and dad, looking bad, etc.). As you write the list, you're forming a hierarchy of items so you can deal first with the anxiety-provokers that bug you most. Very often, taking care of the major items from the top of the list goes a long way toward relieving overall testing anxiety. You probably won't have to bother with the stuff you placed last.

TAKE STOCK OF YOUR STRENGTHS AND WEAKNESSES

Take one minute to list the areas of the SAT or any other test that you are good at. They can be general ("world history") or specific ("Nevada from 1850 to 1875"). Put down as many as you can think of, and if possible, time yourself. Write for the entire time; don't stop writing until you've reached the one minute stopping point.

Strong Test Subjects

_____

_____

_____

_____

_____

_____

Next, take one minute to list areas of the test you're not so good at, just plain bad at, have failed at, or keep failing at. Again, keep it to one minute, and continue writing until you reach the cutoff. Don't be afraid to identify and write down your weak spots! In all probability, as you do both lists you'll find you are strong in some areas and not so strong in others. Taking stock of your assets _and_ liabilities lets you know the areas you don't have to worry about, and the ones that will demand extra attention and effort.

Weak Test Subjects

_____

_____

_____

_____

_____

_____

Now, go back to the "good" list, and expand it for two minutes. Take the general items on that first list and make them more specific; take the specific items and expand them into more general conclusions. Naturally, if anything new comes to mind jot it down. Focus all of your attention and effort on your strengths. Don't underestimate yourself or your abilities. Give yourself full credit. At the same time, don't list strengths you don't really have; you'll only be fooling yourself.

Expanding from general to specific might go as follows. If you listed "world history" as a broad topic you feel strong in, you would then narrow your focus to include areas of this subject about which you are particularly knowledgeable. Your areas of strength might include modern European history, the events leading up to World War I, the Bolshevik revolution, etc. You could then break these general categories down to specific areas you know really well. World War I includes the socioeconomic conditions, politics, the rising discontent and rebellion of the population, and all the other factors and events that led up to Archduke Ferdinand becoming an assassin's target.

Suppose your list includes a narrow topic, such as the history of the state of Nevada, 1850 to 1875. Expanding this item from the specific to the overall could include: a chronology of gold and silver mining in the state, how mining production affected both the state and federal economies, harm to the environment because of mining and smelting, and so on, in an ever expanding range of connected issues.

Whatever you know comfortably (that is, almost as well as you know the back of your hand) goes on your "good" list. Okay. You've got the picture. Now, get ready, check your starting time, and start writing down items on your expanded "good" list below.

Strong Test Subjects: An Expanded List

_____

_____

_____

_____

_____

_____

After you've stopped, check your time. Did you find yourself going beyond the two minutes allotted? Did you write down more things than you thought you knew? Is it possible you know more than you've given yourself credit for? Could that mean you've found a number of areas in which you feel strong?

You just took an active step toward helping yourself. Notice any increased feelings of confidence? Enjoy them.

Here's another way to think about your writing exercise. Every area of strength and confidence you can identify is much like having a reserve of solid gold at Fort Knox. You'll be able to draw on your reserves as you need them, and you can use your reserves to solve difficult questions, maintain confidence, and keep test stress and anxiety at a distance. The encouraging thing is that every time you recognize another area of strength, succeed at coming up with a solution, or get a good score on a test, you increase your reserves. And, there is absolutely no limit to how much self-confidence you can have or how good you can feel about yourself.

IMAGINE YOURSELF SUCCEEDING

This next little group of exercises is both physical and mental. It's a natural followup to what you've just accomplished with your lists.

First, get yourself into a comfortable sitting position in a quiet setting. Wear loose clothes. If you wear glasses, take them off. Then, close your eyes and breathe in a deep, satisfying breath of air. Really fill your lungs until your rib cage is fully expanded and you can't take in any more. Then, exhale the air completely. Imagine you're blowing out a candle with your last little puff of air. Do this two or three more times, filling your lungs to their maximum and emptying them totally. Keep your eyes closed, comfortably but not tightly. Let your body sink deeper into the chair as you become even more comfortable.

 FORCING RELAXATION IS LIKE ASKING YOURSELF TO FLAP YOUR ARMS AND FLY. YOU CAN'T DO IT, AND EVERY PUSH AND PROD ONLY GETS YOU MORE FRUSTRATED. RELAXATION IS SOMETHING

YOU DON'T WORK AT. YOU SIMPLY LET IT HAPPEN.
THINK ABOUT IT. WHEN WAS THE LAST TIME YOU
TRIED TO FORCE YOURSELF TO GO TO SLEEP, AND
IT WORKED?

With your eyes shut you can notice something very interesting. You're no longer dealing with the worrisome stuff going on in the world outside of you. Now you can concentrate on what happens inside you. The more you recognize your own physical reactions to stress and anxiety, the more you can do about them. You may not realize it, but you've begun to regain a sense of being in control.

Let images begin to form on the "viewing screens" on the back of your eyelids. You're experiencing visualizations from the place in your mind that makes pictures. Allow the images to come easily and naturally; don't force them. Imagine yourself in a relaxing situation. It might be in a special place you've visited before or one you've read about. It can be a fictional location that you create in your imagination, but a real-life memory of a place or situation you know is usually better. Make it as detailed as possible and notice as much as you can.

If you don't see this relaxing place sharply or in living color, it doesn't mean the exercise won't work for you. Some people can visualize in great detail, while others get only a sense of an image. What's important is not how sharp the details or colors, but how well you're able to manipulate the images. If you can conjure up finely detailed images, great. If you only have a faint sense of the images, that's okay—you'll still experience all the benefits of the exercise.

Think about the sights, the sounds, the smells, even the tastes and textures associated with your relaxing situation. See and feel yourself in this special place. Say you're special place is the beach, for example. Feel how warm the sand is. Are you lying on a blanket, or sitting up and looking out at the water? Hear the waves hitting the shore, and the occasional seagull. Feel a comfortable breeze. If you're special place is a garden or park, look up and see the way sunlight filters through the trees. Smell your favorite flowers. Hear some chimes gently playing and birds chirping.

Stay focused on the images as you sink farther back into your chair. Breathe easily and naturally. You might have the sensations of any stress or tension draining from your muscles and flowing downward, out your feet and away from you.

Take a moment to check how you're feeling. Notice how comfortable you've become. Imagine how much easier it would be if you could take the test feeling this relaxed and in this state of ease. You've coupled the images of your special place with sensations of comfort and relaxation. You've also found a way to become relaxed simply by visualizing your own safe, special place.

Now, close your eyes and start remembering a real-life situation in which you did well on a test. If you can't come up with one, remember a situation in which you did something (academic or otherwise) that you were really proud of—a genuine accomplishment. Make the memory as detailed as possible. Think about the sights, the sounds, the smells, even the tastes associated with this remembered experience. Remember how confident you felt as you accomplished your goal. Now start thinking about the upcoming test. Keep your thoughts and feelings in line with that prior, successful experience. Don't make comparisons between them. Just imagine taking the upcoming test with the same feelings of confidence and relaxed control.

This exercise is a great way to bring the test down to earth. You should practice this exercise often, especially when the prospect of taking the exam starts to bum you out. The more you practice it, the more effective the exercise will be for you.

WHAT DO YOU WANT TO ACCOMPLISH IN THE TIME REMAINING?

The whole point to this next exercise is sort of like checking out a used car you might want to buy. You'd want to know up front what the car's weak points are, right? Knowing that influences your whole shopping-for-a-used-car campaign. So it is with your conquering-test-stress campaign: Knowing what your weak points are ahead of time helps you prepare.

 DON'T FORGET THAT YOUR HIGH SCHOOL PROBABLY HAS COUNSELING AVAILABLE. IF YOU CAN'T CONQUER THE STRESS ON YOUR OWN, MAKE AN APPOINTMENT AT THE COUNSELING OFFICE. THEY ARE THERE TO HELP YOU.

So let's get back to the list of your weak points. Take two minutes to expand it just as you did with your "good" list. Be honest with your-self without going overboard. It's an accurate appraisal of the test areas that give you troubles. So, pick up your pencil, check the clock, and start writing.

Weak Test Subjects: An Expanded List

_____

_____

_____

_____

_____

_____

_____

_____

How did you do? Were you able to keep writing for the full two minutes? Has making this "weak" list helped you become more clear about the specific areas you need to address?

Facing your weak spots gives you some distinct advantages. It helps a lot to find out where you need to spend extra effort. Increased exposure to tough material makes it more familiar and less intimidating. (After all, we mostly fear what we don't know and are probably afraid to face.) You'll feel better about yourself because you're dealing directly with areas of the test that bring on your anxiety. You can't help feeling more confident when you know you're actively strengthening your chances of earning a higher overall score.

EXERCISE YOUR FRUSTRATIONS AWAY

Whether it is jogging, walking, biking, mild aerobics, pushups, or a pickup basketball game, physical exercise is a very effective way to stimulate both your mind and body and to improve your ability to think and concentrate. A surprising number of students get out of the habit of regular exercise, ironically because they're spending so much time prepping for the exam. Also, sedentary people—this is medical fact—get less oxygen to the blood and hence to the head than active people. You can live fine with a little less oxygen; you just can't think as well.

Any big test is a bit like a race. Thinking clearly at the end is just as important as having a quick mind early on. If you can't sustain your energy level in the last sections of the exam, there's too good a chance you could blow it. You need a fit body that can weather the demands any big exam puts on you. Along with a good diet and adequate sleep, exercise is an important part of keeping yourself in fighting shape and thinking clearly for the long haul.

There's another thing that happens when students don't make exercise an integral part of their test preparation. Like any organism in nature, you operate best if all your "energy systems" are in balance. Studying uses a lot of energy, but it's all mental. When you take a study break, do something active instead of raiding the fridge or vegging-out in front of the TV. Take a five- to ten-minute activity break for every 50 or 60 minutes that you study. The physical exertion gets your body into the act which helps to keep your mind and body in sync. Then, when you finish studying for the night and hit the sack you won't lie there, tense and unable to sleep, because your head is overtired and your body wants to pump iron or run a marathon.

One warning about exercise, however: It's not a good idea to exercise vigorously right before you go to bed. This could easily cause sleep onset problems. For the same reason, it's also not a good idea to study right up to bedtime. Make time for a "buffer period" before you go to bed: For 30 to 60 minutes, just take a hot shower, meditate, simply veg out.

Get High . . . Naturally

Exercise can give you a natural high, which is the only kind of high you can afford right now. Using drugs (prescription or recreational) specifically to prepare for and take a big test is definitely self-defeating. Except for the drugs that occur naturally in your brain, every drug has major drawbacks—and a false sense of security is one of them.

Let's say while studying you find yourself getting tired, and you pop some kind of upper to stay alert. You're just wasting your time. Amphetamines make it hard to retain information. So you'll stay awake, but you probably won't remember much of what you read. And, taking an upper before you take the test could really mess things up. You're already going to be a little anxious and hyper; adding a strong stimulant could easily push you over the edge into panic. Remember, a little anxiety is a good thing. The adrenaline that gets pumped into your bloodstream helps you stay alert and think more clearly. But, too much anxiety and you can't think straight at all.

 To reduce stress you should eat fruits and vegetables (raw is best, or just lightly

STEAMED OR NUKED), LOW-FAT PROTEIN SUCH AS
FISH, SKINLESS POULTRY, BEANS, AND LEGUMES
(LIKE LENTILS), OR WHOLE GRAINS SUCH AS
BROWN RICE, WHOLE WHEAT BREAD AND PASTAS
(NO BLEACHED FLOUR). DON'T EAT REFINED
SUGAR—SWEET, HIGH-FAT SNACKS (SIMPLE
CARBOHYDRATES LIKE SUGAR MAKE STRESS
WORSE, AND FATTY FOODS LOWER YOUR
IMMUNITY) OR SALTY FOODS (THEY CAN DEPLETE
POTASSIUM, WHICH YOU NEED FOR NERVE
FUNCTIONS).

Mild stimulants, such as coffee, cola, or over-the-counter caffeine pills can sometimes help as you study, since they keep you alert. On the down side, they can also lead to agitation, restlessness, and insomnia. Some people can drink a pot of high-octane coffee and sleep like a baby. Others have one cup and start to vibrate. It all depends on your tolerance for caffeine.

Alchohol and other depressants lead to the inevitable hangover/crash, fuzzy thinking, and a lousy sense of judgment. These are not going to help you ace the test.

Instead, go for endorphins—the "natural morphine." Endorphins have no side effects and they're free—you've already got them in your brain. It just takes some exercise to release them. Running around on the basketball court, bicycling, swimming, aerobics, powerwalking—these activities, cause endorphins to occupy certain spots in your brain's neural synapses. In addition, exercise develops staying power and increases the oxygen transfer to your brain.

TAKE A DEEP BREATH . . .

Here's another natural route to relaxation and invigoration. It's a classic isometric exercise that you can do whenever you get stressed out—just before the test begins, even *during* the test. It's very simple and takes just a few minutes.

Close your eyes. Starting with your eyes and—*without holding your breath*—gradually tighten every muscle in your body (but not to the point of pain) in the following sequence:

1. Close your eyes tightly.
2. Squeeze your nose and mouth together so that your whole face is scrunched up. (If it makes you self-conscious to do this in the test room, skip the face-scrunching part.)
3. Pull your chin into your chest, and pull your shoulders together.
4. Tighten your arms to your body, then clench your fists.
5. Pull in your stomach.
6. Squeeze your thighs and buttocks together, and tighten your calves.
7. Stretch your feet, then curl your toes (watch out for cramping in this part).

At this point, every muscle should be tightened. Now, relax your body, one part at a time, *in reverse order*, starting with your toes. Let the tension drop out of each muscle. The entire process might take five minutes from start to finish (maybe a couple of minutes during the test). This clenching and unclenching exercise should help you to feel very relaxed.

. . . AND KEEP BREATHING

Conscious attention to breathing is an excellent way of managing that SAT test stress (or any stress, for that matter). The majority of people who get into trouble during tests take shallow breaths. They breathe using only their upper chests and shoulder muscles, and may even hold their breath for long periods of time. Conversely, the test-taker who by accident or design keeps breathing normally and rhythmically is likely to be more relaxed and in better control during the entire test experience.

So, now is the time to get into the habit of relaxed breathing. Do the next exercise to learn to breathe in a natural, easy rhythm. By the way, this is another technique you can use during the test to collect your thoughts and ward off excess stress. The entire exercise should take no more than three to five minutes.

With your eyes still closed, breathe in slowly and deeply through your nose. Hold the breath for a bit, and then release it through your mouth. The key is to breathe slowly and deeply by using your diaphragm (the big band of muscle that spans your body just above your waist) to draw air in and out naturally and effortlessly. Breathing with your diaphragm encourages relaxation and helps minimize tension.

As you breathe, imagine that colored air is flowing into your lungs. Choose any color you like, from a single color to a rainbow. With each breath, the air fills your body from the top of your head to the tips of your toes. Continue inhaling the colored air until it occupies every part of you, bones and muscles included. Once you have completely filled yourself with the colored air, picture an opening somewhere on your body, either natural or imagined. Now, with each breath you exhale, some of the colored air will pass out the opening and leave your body. The level of the air (much like the water in a glass as it is emptied) will begin to drop. It will descend progressively lower, from your head down to your feet. As you continue to exhale the colored air, watch the level go lower and lower, farther and farther down your body. As the last of the colored air passes out of the opening, the level will drop down to your toes and disappear. Stay quiet for just a moment. Then notice how relaxed and comfortable you feel.

THUMBS UP FOR MEDITATION

Once relegated to the fringes of the medical world, meditation, biofeedback, and hypnosis are increasingly recommended by medical researchers to reduce pain from headaches, back problems—even cancer. Think of what these powerful techniques could do for your test-related stress and anxiety.

Effective meditation is based primarily on two relaxation methods you've already learned: body awareness and breathing. A couple of different meditation techniques follow. Experience them both, and choose the one that works best for you.

BREATH MEDITATION

Make yourself comfortable, either sitting or lying down. For this meditation you can keep your eyes open or closed. You're going to concentrate on your breathing. The goal of the meditation is to notice everything you can about your breath as it enters and leaves your body. Take three to five breaths each time you practice the meditation, which should take about a minute for the entire procedure.

Take a deep breath and hold it for five to ten seconds. When you exhale, let the breath out very slowly. Feel the tension flowing out of you along with the breath that leaves your body. Pay close attention to the air as it flows in and out of your nostrils. Observe how cool it is as you inhale and how warm your breath is when you exhale. As you expel the air, say a cue word such as "calm" or "relax" to yourself. Once you've exhaled all the air from your lungs, start the next long, slow inhale. Notice how relaxed feelings increase as you slowly exhale and again hear your cue words.

MANTRA MEDITATION

For this type of meditation experience you'll need a mental device (a mantra), a passive attitude (don't try to do anything), and a position in which you can be comfortable. You've going to focus your total attention on a mantra you create. It should be emotionally neutral, repetitive, and monotonous, and your aim is to fully occupy your mind with it. Furthermore, you want to do the meditation passively, with no goal in your head of how relaxed you're supposed to be. This is a great way to prepare for studying or taking the test. It clears your head of extraneous thoughts and gets you focused and at ease.

Sit comfortably and close your eyes. Begin to relax by letting your body go limp. Create a relaxed mental attitude and know there's no need for you to force anything. You're simply going to let something happen. Breathe through your nose. Take calm, easy breaths and as you exhale, say your mantra (*one, ohhm, aah, soup*—whatever is emotionally neutral for you) to yourself. Repeat the mantra each time you breathe out. Let feelings of relaxation grow as you focus on the mantra and your slow breathing. Don't worry if your mind wanders. Simply return to the mantra and continue letting go. Experience this meditation for ten to fifteen minutes.

NEVER TRY TO FORCE RELAXATION. YOU'LL ONLY
GET FRUSTRATED AND MORE TENSE.

QUICK TIPS FOR THE DAYS JUST BEFORE THE EXAM

- The best test takers do less and less as exam day approaches. Taper off on your study schedule and take it easy on yourself. You want to be relaxed and ready on test day. Give yourself time off, especially the evening before the exam. By that time, if you've studied well, everything you need to know is firmly stored in your memory banks.

- Positive self-talk can be extremely liberating and invigorating, especially as the test looms closer. Tell yourself things such as, "I *choose* to take this test" rather than "I *have* to"; "I *will* do well" rather than "I *hope* things go well"; "I *can*" rather than, "I *cannot*." Be aware of negative, self-defeating thoughts and images and immediately counter any you become aware of. Replace them with affirming statements that encourage your self-esteem and confidence. Create and practice doing visualizations that build on your positive statements.

- Get your act together sooner rather than later. Have everything (including choice of clothing) laid out days in advance. Most important, *know where the test will be held and the easiest, quickest way to get there.* You will gain great peace of mind if you know that all the little details—gas in the car, directions, etc.—are firmly in your control before test day.

- Experience the test site a few days in advance. This is very helpful if you are especially anxious. If at all possible, find out what room your part of the alphabet is assigned to, and try to sit there (by yourself) for a while. Better yet, bring some practice material and do at least a section or two, if not an entire practice test, in that room. In this case, familiarity doesn't breed contempt, it generates comfort and confidence.

- Forego any practice on the day before the test. It's in your best interest to marshal your physical and psychological resources for twenty-four hours or so. Even race horses are kept in the paddock and treated like princes the day before a race. Keep the upcoming test out of your consciousness; go to a movie, take a pleasant hike, or just relax. Don't eat junk food or tons of sugar. And—of course—get plenty of rest the night before. Just don't go to bed too early. It's hard to fall asleep earlier than your used to, and you don't want to lie there thinking about the test.

 WHEN YOU DRESS ON TEST DAY, DO IT IN LOOSE LAYERS. THAT WAY YOU'LL BE PREPARED NO MATTER WHAT THE TEMPERATURE OF THE ROOM IS. (AN UNCOMFORTABLE TEMPERATURE WILL JUST DISTRACT YOU FROM THE JOB AT HAND.) AND, IF YOU HAVE AN ITEM OF CLOTHING THAT YOU TEND TO FEEL "LUCKY" OR CONFIDENT IN—A SHIRT, A PAIR OF JEANS, WHATEVER—WEAR IT. A LITTLE TOTEM COULDN'T HURT.

STRESS TIPS

- Don't work in a messy or cramped area. Before you sit down to study, clear yourself a nice, open space. And make sure you have books, paper, pencils—whatever tools you will need—within easy reach before you sit down to study.

- Don't study on your bed, especially if you have problems with insomnia. Your mind may start to associate the bed with work, and make it even harder for you to fall asleep.
- A lamp with a 75-watt bulb is optimal for studying. But don't keep it so close t that you create a glare.
- If you want to play music, keep it low and in the background. Music with a regular, mathematical rhythm— reggae, for example—aids the learning process. A recording of ocean waves is also soothing.

HANDLING STRESS DURING THE TEST

The biggest stress monster will be test day itself. Fear not; there are methods of quelling your stress during the test.

- Keep moving forward instead of getting bogged down in a difficult question, game, or passage. You don't have to get everything right to achieve a fine score. So, don't linger out of desperation on a question that is going nowhere even after you've spent considerable time on it. The best test-takers skip (temporarily) difficult material in search of the easier stuff. They mark the ones that require extra time and thought. This strategy buys time and builds confidence so you can handle the tough stuff later.
- Don't be thrown if other test takers seem to be working more busily and furiously than you are. Continue to spend your time patiently but doggedly thinking through your answers; it's going to lead to higher-quality test taking and better results. Don't mistake the other people's sheer activity for progress and higher scores.

- *Keep breathing!* Weak test takers tend to share one major trait: They forget to breathe properly as the test proceeds. They start holding their breath without realizing it, or they breathe erratically or arrhythmically. Improper breathing can hurt hurt your confidence and accuracy. Just as important, it can interfere with clear thinking.

- Some quick isometrics during the test—especially if concentration is wandering or energy is waning—can help. Try this: Put your palms together and press intensely for a few seconds. Concentrate on the tension you feel through your palms, wrists, forearms, and up into your biceps and shoulders. Then, quickly release the pressure. Feel the difference as you let go. Focus on the warm relaxation that floods through the muscles. Now you're ready to return to the task.

- Here's another isometric exercise that will relieve tension in both your neck and eye muscles. Slowly rotate your head from side to side, turning your head and eyes to look as far back over each shoulder as you can. Feel the muscles stretch on one side of your neck as they contract on the other. Repeat this processive times in each direction.

With what you've just learned here, you're armed and ready to do battle with the SAT—or any other test. This book and your studies will give you the information you'll need to answer the questions. It's all firmly planted in your mind. You also know how to deal with any excess tension that might come along, both when you're studying for and taking the exam. You've experienced everything you need to tame your test anxiety and stress. You *are* going to get a great score.

Want more information about our services, products, or the nearest Kaplan center?

1 **Call our nationwide toll-free numbers:**

1-800-KAP-TEST for information on our live courses, private tutoring and admissions consulting
1-800-KAP-ITEM for information on our products
1-888-KAP-LOAN* for information on student loans

2 **Connect with us in cyberspace:**

On AOL, keyword:"Kaplan"
On the World Wide Web, go to: http://www.kaplan.com
Via e-mail: info@kaplan.com

3 **Write to:**

Kaplan Educational Centers
888 Seventh Avenue
New York, NY 10106

About KAPLAN

Educational Centers

Kaplan Educational Centers is one of the nation's premier education companies, providing individuals with a full range of resources to achieve their educational and career goals. Kaplan, celebrating its 60th anniversary, is a wholly-owned subsidiary of The Washington Post Company.

TEST PREPARATION & ADMISSIONS

Kaplan's nationally-recognized test prep courses cover more than 20 standardized tests, including entrance exams for secondary school, college and graduate school as well as foreign language and professional licensing exams. In addition, Kaplan offers private tutoring and comprehensive, one-to-one admissions and application advice for students applying to graduate school.

SCORE! EDUCATIONAL CENTERS

SCORE! after-school learning centers help students in grades K-8 build academic skills, confidence and goal-setting skills in a motivating, sports-oriented environment. Kids use a cutting-edge, interactive curriculum that continually assesses and adapts to their academic needs and learning style. Enthusiastic Academic Coaches serve as positive role models, creating a high-energy atmosphere where learning is exciting and fun for kids. With nearly 40 centers today, SCORE! continues to open new centers nationwide.

KAPLAN LEARNING SERVICES

Kaplan Learning Services provides customized assessment, education and training programs to K-12 schools, universities and businesses to help students and employees reach their educational and career goals.

KAPLAN INTERNATIONAL

Kaplan serves international students and professionals in the U.S. through Access America, a series of intensive English language programs, and LCP International Institute, a leading provider of intensive English language programs at on-campus centers in California, Washington and New York. Kaplan and LCP offer specialized services to sponsors including placement at top American universities, fellowship management, academic monitoring and reporting and financial administration.

KAPLOAN

Students can get key information and advice about educational loans for college and graduate school through **KapLoan** (Kaplan Student Loan Information Program). Through an affiliation with one of the nation's largest student loan providers, **KapLoan** helps direct students and their families through the often bewildering financial aid process.

KAPLAN PUBLISHING

Kaplan Books, a joint imprint with Simon & Schuster, publishes books in test preparation, admissions, education,career development and life skills; Kaplan and *Newsweek* jointly publish the highly successful guides, **How to Get Into College** and **How to Choose a Career & Graduate School**. SCORE! and *Newsweek* have teamed up to publish **How to Help Your Child Suceed in School**.

Kaplan InterActive delivers award-winning, high quality educational products and services including Kaplan's best-selling **Higher Score** test-prep software and sites on the internet **(http://www.kaplan.com)** and America Online. Kaplan and Cendant Software are jointly developing, marketing and distributing educational software for the kindergarten through twelfth grade retail and school markets.

KAPLAN CAREER SERVICES

Kaplan helps students and graduates find jobs through Kaplan Career Services, the leading provider of career fairs in North America. The division includes **Crimson & Brown Associates**, the nation's leading diversity recruiting and publishing firm, and **The Lendman Group and Career Expo**, both of which help clients identify highly sought-after technical personnel and sales and marketing professionals.

COMMUNITY OUTREACH

Kaplan provides educational resources to thousands of financially disadvantaged students annually, working closely with educational institutions, not-for-profit groups, government agencies and other grass roots organizations on a variety of national and local support programs. Also, Kaplan centers enrich local communities by employing high school, college and graduate students, creating valuable work experiences for vast numbers of young people each year.